PRENTICE-HALL
CONTEMPORARY COMPARATIVE POLITICS SERIES
JOSEPH LaPALOMBARA, Editor

PSYCHOLOGY AND POLITICS
Christian Bay

COMPARATIVE LEGISLATURES
Jean Blondel

COMPARATIVE LEGAL CULTURES
Henry W. Ehrmann

COMPARATIVE URBAN POLITICS
Robert Fried and Francine Rabinovitz

COMPARATIVE CONSTITUTIONALISM
Carl J. Friedrich

COMPARATIVE POLITICAL IDEOLOGIES
Peter Gourevitch

COMPARATIVE REVOLUTIONARY MOVEMENTS
Thomas H. Greene

COMPARATIVE POLITICAL SOCIALIZATION
Timothy M. Hennessey

COMPARATIVE BUREAUCRACY
Martin Landau

THE MILITARY AND POLITICAL DEVELOPMENT
Eric A. Nordlinger

COMPARATIVE POLITICAL ELITES
Robert D. Putnam

COMPARATIVE ELECTIONS AND POLITICAL DEMOCRACY
Douglas W. Rae and Michael Taylor

COMPARATIVE POLITICAL CORRUPTION
James C. Scott

COMPARATIVE POLITICAL VIOLENCE
Fred R. von der Mehden

JAMES C. SCOTT
University of Wisconsin

Prentice-Hall, Inc.,
Englewood Cliffs, N.J.

COMPARATIVE POLITICAL CORRUPTION

COMPARATIVE POLITICAL CORRUPTION
James C. Scott

ISBN: C: 0–13–179036–6
P: 0–13–179028–5

Printed in the United States of America

Library of Congress Catalog Card Number: 75–161461

10 9 8 7 6 5 4 3 2 1

PRENTICE-HALL INTERNATIONAL, INC., London
PRENTICE-HALL OF AUSTRALIA, PTY. LTD., Sydney
PRENTICE-HALL OF CANADA, LTD., Toronto
PRENTICE-HALL OF INDIA PRIVATE LIMITED, New Delhi
PRENTICE-HALL OF JAPAN, INC., Tokyo

CONTENTS

FOREWORD

This volume on political corruption is the first in a series on Contemporary Comparative Politics that has been several years in the planning stage. The series will treat the more enduring as well as the more recent themes, approaches, and problems pertaining to the study of political systems. Combinations of these volumes will permit the instructor to group basic text materials that suit his particular design of a course. In all cases, the volumes are pointed toward the following goals: to illustrate the relationship between theory and method without being theoretically pretentious or methodologically self-conscious; to underline the essential interrelatedness between fact and value or empirical and normative consideration in politics; to inform the reader in brief compass and in ordinary language, free from the jargon and neologisms of modern social science. The final and overriding goal of the series is to show what the comparative political scientist does and why this is an activity of intrinsic interest for the student and considerable utility for society.

The organization of the series is based on a number of assumptions and guidelines that are worth calling to the reader's attention. Foremost among these is that the undergraduate student of comparative politics is less interested in political science than we might hope, but more capable of synthetic analysis than we may imagine. If this is so, then it would be an enormous mistake to pretend to organize an introductory series around one or more half-baked "theories" of politics or political systems—theories that are difficult for even the more hardened members of the profession to digest. It would seem equally debatable whether the undergraduate student has a strong desire to learn in depth the institutional arrangements and workings of any single political system, whether that system be as established as that of Great Britain or as new and exotic as that of Tanzania.

Another major assumption underlying the organization of the series is that the topics included should not reflect a commitment to an institutional or behavioral, normative or empirical approach. If members of the profession are still battling about such things, let them spare undergraduates the arid, scholastic, and essentially unproductive nature of such encounters. The authors of this series are neither bare-facts empiricists nor "cloud-ninety" political moralists; they neither sanctify nor abominate institutional or behavioral analysis but would rather use whatever methods are available to enlighten the reader about important aspects of political life. To emphasize the important is also to be relevant, and our correlative assumption here is that the student who wants political science to be "relevant" does not mean by this that it should be banal, simple-minded, or unsystematic.

Since no series can tell us everything about politics, we have had to choose what we consider to be the important, relevant, and reasonably integrated topics. Such choices are always arbitrary to some extent. However, we have sought to accord attention to certain standard and ubiquitous institutions as well as to newer conceptual and analytical foci that have provoked a good deal of recent research and discussion. Thus, the series will have a volume on Comparative Legal Cultures, but another on Comparative Political Violence; it will include a fine volume on Constitutionalism, and one on Revolutionary Movements.

Given assumptions such as these, it is entirely fitting that the series should be inaugurated by James Scott's volume on political corruption. As the pages that follow will attest, patterns of corruption have been and are associated with political development and nation-building. To focus on this particular aspect of political organization and behavior permits us better to understand how, for instance, Great Britain succeeded as a polity and why Thailand may or may not succeed, given different degrees and patterns of corruption. In any event, we read Scott with great profit if we understand that his discussion of the political machine gives us a better basis for telescoping space and time, thus permitting us to understand the ways in which the political systems of Ghana and India are like or unlike those of the United States or Great Britain. It is, after all, the identification of these differences and similarities and their explanation that constitutes much of what comparative political science is all about.

Volumes to follow this one will represent what we believe is an interesting and useful mosaic that should be appealing to those who teach, those who learn about, and all of those who try to understand politics.

JOSEPH LAPALOMBARA

Rome

PREFACE

The perspective of this book is that corruption, like violence, must be understood as a regular, repetitive, integral part of the operation of most political systems. In practice, this simply means that an analysis of who in a society gets what, when, where, and how that relies exclusively upon an examination of those political acts open to public view would seldom provide an accurate picture of political reality. Recurring acts of violence and corruption are thus more successfully analyzed as normal channels of political activity than as cases of deviant pathology requiring incarceration and/or moral instruction for the perpetrator(s). Just as social banditry and piracy must be viewed as integral parts of many agrarian and maritime economies, so, for example, must vote-buying and "rake-offs" be seen as an integral part of United States urban politics at the turn of the twentieth century. Far from being pathological, patterns of corruption and violence may actually represent channels of political demands without which formal societal arrangements could scarcely survive.

In keeping with this perspective, I have consistently tried to show how patterns of access and exclusion in the formal political apparatus help determine which groups will most likely resort to corruption or violence. Since corruption is a violation of certain rules, the amount and nature of corruption is, in part, determined by those rules. If the rules permit large campaign contributions, they often simply institutionalize a transaction between wealth and power that occurs illegally under a more restrictive set of rules. Given the importance of the existing set of rules to any examination of corruption, I have tried to be sensitive both to how rules serve some people's interests more than others and to differences in rules historically and comparatively.

Although structural conditions and—to a much smaller extent—traditional values common to many poor nations predispose them to high levels of corruption, it is all too easy for the analyst to become mesmerized by such conditions and be blinded to man's capacity to refashion his values and situation. To take the most striking example, the cadre of the National Liberation Front of South Vietnam and the local officials of the Saigon regime are drawn from the same cultural milieu and operate within the same society. From all accounts, however, N.L.F. cadre administer the villages they control with scrupulous attention to N.L.F. regulations, whereas even Saigon's partisans concede that the South Vietnamese administration is generally characterized by dishonesty, malfeasance, and a rapacious attitude toward the local populace. The explanation for this difference in administration clearly lies not so much in coercive capacity but in the ability of the N.L.F. to develop a new system of legitimacy by both symbolic and concrete acts that engender the social sanctions which make that order effective. The obstacles to a noncorrupt political order in less-developed nations are real, but they are not insurmountable.

Much of my analysis reflects the frequently conservative consequences of corruption. Except perhaps where corruption allows the bourgeoisie to buy its way into a previously closed elite, the normal effect of corruption is to cement together a conservative coalition and hold back or cancel out the effects of growing collective demands. Whether the coalition is one between the narrow, nonelected, military/civilian elite and local Chinese business interests, as in Thailand, or between the Indian National Congress and rural elites who control the votes of their clients and tenants, the result is comparable. In this context, my pessimism about the capacity of competitive parliamentary regimes to undertake basic structural reforms is evident throughout much of the text.

Although case material on corruption abounds, it is seldom reliable, and aggregate data are virtually impossible to find or to assemble. For the most part, one is forced to infer what lies below the surface from an analysis of the exposed tip of the iceberg and from the general characteristics of the political system. Inferences in the case of Stuart England or United States cities at the turn of the century can be constructed with some assurance, given the accumulated wealth of case studies and historical analysis. For less-developed nations over the past two decades, the data base is more tenuous. In countries with parliamentary systems we can examine—with appropriate caution—press accounts, campaign charges, court proceedings, and the reports of a number of official commissions of inquiry, in addition to scholarly assessments. For nonparliamentary systems we operate at an even greater disadvantage, except when a regime has been overthrown—and even then the *post hoc* exposures are often distorted in the media to serve the new regime's purposes. I have thus chosen case studies with an eye to the available evidence; when the data was very thin, I have necessarily been more cautious.

Considerations of space and my own limitations are responsible for the absence of any substantive analysis of corruption in the socialist bloc or in Latin America. The material on the socialist bloc is sparse and concerns mainly the informal economic arrangements designed to circumvent the snarls of central planning, which may seem inadequate for a general discussion of corruption in such systems. For Latin America the empirical obstacles are not severe, but my limited knowledge of the area would have precluded my adding anything original to existing studies.

ACKNOWLEDGMENTS

As the author of an eclectic book I have acquired a set of equally eclectic intellectual debts. Among those who kindly took the time to send me comments ranging all the way from encouragement to frontal assaults on my argument are Dorothy and Jim Guyot, Milton Esman, Paul Brass, Fred von der Mehden, Peter Mayer, Gary Brewer, Arnold Heidenheimer, Charles Tilly, Jean Grossholtz, William Sachse, and Carl Lande. Like many others, I have profited from a vigorous tradition of collegial reciprocity among political scientists at the University of Wisconsin. Fred Hayward, Booth Fowler, Crawford Young, Henry Hart, Dennis Dresang, Ken Dolbeare, and Michael Lipsky all gave me their candid criticisms. I am especially obligated to Ed Friedman and Murray Edelman who, by the example of their own work and their criticisms of mine, have helped bring the values I hold and the questions I ask into line in a way that only begins to emerge in this volume. My editor, Joseph LaPalombara, by his insistence on brevity and clarity, has hopefully saved the reader much confusion and repetition. I am thankful to the University of Wisconsin Research Committee and the National Science Foundation Postdoctoral Fellowship program for the time this research required. Finally, Philip Rosenberg, Bill Gudger, Greg Tewksbury, Dick Sullivan, Elizabeth Pringle, Jo Southeran, Ginny Eismon, Marge Kritz, and Carol Shutvet all lent their talents to the preparation of the manuscript. If the final text does not reflect the amazing array of talent I have had at my disposal from the outset, that is my problem.

I am grateful to the editors of *Asian Studies, Comparative Studies in Society and History,* and *The American Political Science Review* for permission to quote from articles of mine which appeared in their journals.

This book is dedicated to my wife Louise, without whose gentle sabotage it would have been completed at least six months earlier. I value her for keeping me as human as possible, not for helping me meet the publisher's schedules.

J. C. S.

CORRUPTION
A GENERAL VIEW
1

CORRUPTION AS A POLITICAL EVENT

This is a book about corruption. There are any number of perspectives from which corruption may be viewed, each with its own questions to ask and each with its own method of answering those questions. An economist, for example, finding that the ruling party of a new nation through its minister of public works exacts 5 to 10 percent in graft on each contract it awards, might want to know how this affects the society's rate of savings, its investment decisions, its pattern of income distribution, or its ability to carry out a five-year development plan. An anthropologist, noticing that a peasant who gets a favorable decision in the local criminal court will express his gratitude by delivering a chicken to the judge's house the next morning, would be interested to know how community values foster or inhibit this sort of corruption, how cultural beliefs about this practice have evolved, or how corruption serves to maintain or disrupt existing social bonds. Most public administration specialists, of course, want to know more about corruption so that they can devise ways to put a stop to it.

The perspective adopted here—with prodigious borrowing from other disciplines—is that of political science, with its own set of questions and theoretical tools. When a political scientist finds that many government actions are heavily influenced by a pattern of bribery or by obligations to close kin and friends, he is likely to ask how this situation affects the distribution of power and authority in the political system, how it distorts the formal declarations of government policy, how it influences the character and composition of the political elite over time. Such questions will be the focus of our analysis when we compare and contrast such diverse forms of corruption as the sale of aristocratic titles in seventeenth-century England, the buying of votes by big-city "machines" in the United States at the turn of this century, and the sale of import licenses by political leaders in Indonesia in the early 1950s.

If the study of corruption teaches us anything at all, it teaches us not to take a political system or a particular regime at its face value. Corruption, after all, may be seen as an informal political system. Whereas party manifestos, general legislation, and policy declarations are the formal façade of the political structure, corruption stands in sharp contrast to these features as an informal political system in its own right. Here coalitions that could not survive the light of day, government decisions that would set off a public outcry, elite behavior that would destroy many a political career are all located. For a few nations this hidden arena is only of marginal importance and, although worthy of study, would not appreciably change an evaluation based on what takes place in public. For most nations at some point in their history, and for many nations today, however, the surreptitious politics of this arena is so decisive that an analysis which ignored it would be not simply inaccurate but completely misleading. How for example, could we have adequately explained the rule of Boss Tweed in New York of the 1890s, the structure of Chiang Kai-shek's Kuomintang Party, the methods of "Papa

Doc" Duvalier in Haiti, or the failure of the parliamentary system in Indonesia without examining corruption? These are perhaps dramatic examples but they alert us to the fact that corruption is frequently an integral part of the political system—a part which we ignore only at our great peril.

As an informal political system, corruption often has similar causes, patterns, and consequences in different political contexts. We can discern similar forces at work, for instance, in the bribe a Chinese peasant might have paid a mandarin bureaucrat to escape the annual head tax a century ago and in the money a Ghanaian farmer gives a tax official today to underassess his annual income. The loan a prominent merchant might have given the English king in the seventeenth century in return for being awarded the salt monopoly is comparable in many ways to the campaign contributions a parking-meter salesman gives an American city mayor in exchange for the promise of a postelection supply contract. Pork-barrel projects serve similar functions in India and in Italy. In fact, a central thesis of this book is that patterns of corruption can be related to the character of the political system and to the nature and rate of socioeconomic change in a way that suggests meaningful parallels not only between western and nonwestern nations but also between regimes that have long since disappeared and regimes that thrive today. The pattern of corruption in a particular nation at a given point in time is in one sense unique. But from a wider perspective, it reflects a configuration of political institutions, popular values, and social strains that many other countries have experienced in greater or lesser degree.

DEFINITION

Before considering problems in the comparative study of corruption we must establish a working definition that will encompass much of the behavior we commonly have in mind when we use the term and yet be sharp enough to establish clear boundaries to our analysis.

Corruption, we would all agree, involves a deviation from certain standards of behavior. The first question which arises is, What criteria shall we use to establish those standards? Broadly speaking, there are three criteria from which to choose: the public interest, public opinion, and legal norms. The referents of all three overlap considerably, but each implies a distinct analytical focus and each raises certain operational problems.

On the basis of workability alone, the public interest and public opinion criteria pose great difficulties. A standard of "public interest" would require an unambiguous definition of the public interest so that acts could be classified according to whether they served that "interest" or not. Any proposed definition of the public interest would find little acceptance simply because it would represent an attempt to resolve an essentially normative or ideological question by definition! Moreover, we can imagine many acts we would commonly call corruption—e.g., placing destitute immigrants illegally on the city payroll—that could be considered in the public interest, just as we can imagine acts against the public interest—e.g., the legislative creation of tax loopholes for the very rich—which, however much they smack of favoritism, are not commonly seen as corrupt.[1]

An alternative solution is to ask whether the public considers an act corrupt and to use the public's judgment as the definitional criterion. We could, in fact, determine how the public labeled different acts, but we would undoubtedly find opinion divided or ambiguous in many instances. Should we then take the majority's view, the consensus among the most powerful, the "best" opinion, or what? The choice would be arbitrary and each alternative creates its own problems.[2]

Given these difficulties, it seems preferable not to adopt either the public interest or public opinion as definitional criteria. By purposely excluding both considerations from the definition itself, we can then *empirically* ask how a corrupt act affects the public and how it is regarded by the public.

The third alternative of relying heavily on legal norms in defining corruption, while it too has shortcomings, seems the most satisfactory alternative. Subject to further clarification, we may define corruption as:

> *behavior which deviates from the formal duties of a public role (elective or appointive) because of private-regarding (personal, close family, private clique) wealth or status gains: or violates rules against the exercise of certain types of private-regarding influence [Nye, 1967, p. 416].* [3]

As corruption generally involves a two-party transaction, the initial portion of the definition refers to the person(s) in the transaction who occupies a public role and the last portion to the person(s) acting in a private capacity.

Two terms in this definition require further comment. First, the meaning of "private-regarding" should not be too narrowly conceived. Consider, for example, the politician who, from motives of loyalty, illegally diverts public funds to his ethnic association or political party.[4] Although the group favored is broader than a private clique, nevertheless we would normally consider such a deviation from a public role to be corrupt. The act in point is not

[1] For a definition that does build on a notion of "the common interest," see Rogow and Lasswell, 1963, p. 132.

[2] What the public thinks, of course, does make a difference in the incidence and consequences of most corrupt acts. Arnold Heidenheimer (1970, pp. 26–28), in his careful discussion of this problem, distinguishes between "white," "grey," and "black" corruption according to the intensity and unanimity of public disapproval.

[3] The last portion of Nye's definition is taken from Banfield, 1961, p. 315.

[4] Of course, if his loyalty to such a group leads him to *legally* favor it through his official patronage powers or policy decisions, he may be seen as unduly partisan, but not as corrupt by our definition.

merely hypothetical, for it has occurred in America and in underdeveloped nations with some frequency. Second, the meaning of "behavior" ought to be clarified. Corruption frequently involves a *failure* to enforce laws or invoke sanctions that are applicable to a situation (e.g., a policeman's accepting money in return for overlooking illegal gambling) and, for this reason, the term "behavior" must also cover the *willful* failure to act in accordance with the formal duties of a public role.

One should have a clear conception of what the definition excludes as well as of what it includes. For example, a powerful lobby's ability to secure passage of a law that greatly benefits its members does not in itself constitute corruption unless it can also be shown that the lobby bribed legislators or otherwise violated formal norms. In a more general sense, our conception of corruption does not cover political systems that are, in Aristotelian terms, "corrupt" in that they systematically serve the interests of special groups or sectors. A given regime may be biased and repressive; it may consistently favor the interests, say, of the aristocracy, big business, a single ethnic group, or a single region while it represses other demands, but it is not *ipso facto* corrupt unless these ends are accomplished by breaching the formal norms of office. Although we will talk of the incidence of corrupt acts under a particular regime or within a certain sector, we use the term to refer to behavior—to acts—and not to individuals, groups, or regimes.

As it stands, our definition covers most behavior commonly referred to in discussions of corruption in public life. Most abuses of public power for private ends would fall into its net. It includes acts as diverse as a peasant's minute payment to a public hospital orderly to ensure his seeing a doctor and a large firm's generous bribe to a politician in return for his fiddling with the tax laws to its advantage. It includes favors done from motives of personal loyalty or kinship as well as favors done for cash.

COMPARATIVE PROBLEMS

On *a priori* grounds a legalistic definition of corruption has much to recommend it, both because the illegality of the behavior has become a part of contemporary notions of corruption and because of the very real effect of the legal environment on the nature, extent, and consequences of such behavior. The use of formal norms, however, raises some serious problems for historical comparison and for comparisons between different nations. Three such central problems concern:

1. the danger of implicitly giving normative value to whatever standards of official conduct happen to prevail and thereby failing to treat corruption as an integral part of politics;
2. the difficulty of comparing nations (or a single nation at two points in time) when their formal norms of office holding are quite divergent;
3. the distortion introduced when we compare a nation with a small public sector to one with a large public sector.

RECOGNIZING NORMS AS A PRODUCT OF POLITICS

In taking existing formal norms for public officials as a standard against which to gauge corruption, we must indeed be on guard lest we seem to celebrate that standard as a desirable one. At a superficial level, this simply means that we must avoid the *a priori* moral judgments that the term "corruption" popularly connotes. Somewhat more profoundly, it requires us to recognize that formal norms of behavior are always part of an institutional order which, in turn, reflects the existing distribution of power within a society. These formal norms operate to the advantage of some groups and to the disadvantage of others. Sometimes these advantages are obvious, as in traditional systems where certain posts are only open to the aristocracy; at other times advantages are less obvious, as in the advantages "due process" gives to those with the financial resources to fight prolonged legal battles. In our analysis, therefore, we will try to demonstrate how the formal institutional framework often serves the interests of special sectors and to see if one can predict patterns of corruption by examining the forms of discrimination built into the formal framework.

A closely related problem in the comparative study of corruption involves not so much a question of formal analysis as a question of our scope of inquiry. As much as possible, we shall try to view corruption as a special case of political influence—a case that must be seen in the context of the distribution of power in society and the character of regime institutions. When we examine specific regimes such as England under the early Stuarts, or India under the Congress Party, we will attempt to show how the pattern of corruption is related in each case to the values and institutions of both the elite and the society as a whole. In concrete terms, this means treating an American urban political "machine," in which corruption is commonly rife, *as part of an entire system* of electoral and financial influence in which legal patronage, pork-barrel legislation, and lax regulation of city-based business interests are also important features. Thus, because an adequate understanding of corruption generally requires a grasp of an entire network of influence, we shall try to deal with corruption in a way that embeds it contextually in a broader analysis of a regime's political dynamics.

COMPARING NORMS

The second, and most serious, difficulty arising from the use of formal norms to define corruption is that it seems to rule out some historical comparisons. An example will illustrate the dilemma. If we wanted to compare corruption in seventeenth-century France with corruption in twentieth-century France, a legal perspective would make our task difficult. The sale of state offices in seventeenth-century France would not come under our definition of corruption, whereas the same act in twentieth-century France—or the United States—would. The behavior seems the same; only the legal context has changed. Nor would the use of a "public opinion" criterion here instead of the legal standard solve the dilemma, inasmuch as the sale of office in seventeenth-century France was neither illegal nor frowned upon, except by the old nobility who resented the nouveau riche office holder. In a similar vein, the alarm among the Dutch at increased corruption in colonial Indonesia in the nineteenth century did not result from a change in what colonial officials were doing, but rather from a shift in the values and public law being applied to such behavior in Holland (cf. Wertheim, 1965, p. 111).

We face the same problem in comparing practices in eighteenth-century Europe with identical practices in new states today. The new states, for the most part, have adopted the full panoply of laws that emerged from the long political struggle for reform in the west. Considering only political patronage jobs, the Indian, Malaysian, or Nigerian politician finds himself denied by law many of the spoils that legally aided the growth of political parties in England and America. The *Report of the Committee on Prevention of Corruption* (1964, p. 6), an official Indian report, explicitly recognizes the difficulty of comparing the severity of bureaucratic corruption in India with that of eighteenth-century England because the legal framework under which India operates was not yet established in England at that time. Patronage in contemporary India and in eighteenth-century England may seem to serve much the same purpose but, from the legal perspective, the former is corruption whereas the latter is not.

The difficulty here simply serves to highlight the fact that much corruption is in a real sense a product of the late eighteenth and nineteenth centuries. Only the rise of the modern nation-state, with its mass participation, broadly representative bodies, and elaborate civil service codes, signaled the transformation of the view of government office, and even kingship, from a private right into a public responsibility.

How, then, can we handle historical comparisons? If, for example, we wanted to compare the practice of bribing to gain appointment to the bureaucracy in traditional England with the same practice in modern England, we could classify such an act as corrupt in the modern period but not in the traditional period, where it often occurred openly and legally. We will want, nonetheless, to compare *practices* that are corrupt only by modern standards and ask what their causes are in different periods, how they affect the composition of the elite, and so forth. If nepotism or bribery have similar causes and consequences in early France as in contemporary India, that is an important subject for analysis, notwithstanding the fact that legal codes and public standards have changed so much that what was tolerated (not corrupt) in early France is now forbidden by law (corrupt) in India. For our comparative purposes, then, we will refer to pre-nineteenth-century practices which only became "corrupt" in the nineteenth century as "*proto-corruption.*"[5] This convention will allow us to analyze the comparative causes and effects of similar behavior while recognizing that such earlier practices did not contravene the existing norms of official conduct and thus cannot be considered corruption as we have chosen to use the term.

AVOIDING DISTORTION IN COMPARING NORMS

The difficulties for comparative historical studies posed by evolving legal standards do not so seriously affect contemporary cross-national comparisons. Inasmuch as the legal standards of public conduct in less developed countries are substantially the same as those in use in the west—a colonial heritage—the terms of comparison are roughly similar.[6]

We do face a difficulty, however, in comparing two or more nations where the relative size of the public sector varies widely. Ever since the distinction between acting in a public capacity and acting in a private capacity became generally accepted in the nineteenth century, the formal standards of behavior have been more demanding for the public sector than for the private sector. The owner of a private firm may appoint his unqualified son-in-law assistant vice president and, although he may regret the appointment financially and be accused of bad taste, he remains quite within the law.[7] Should a politician or bureaucrat, however, do the same thing he runs the risk of legal prosecution.

Whether a given act takes place within the public sector or outside it thus makes a substantial difference in whether it meets the legal criteria of corruption. Restraints in the case of the public sector are the responsibility of legislatures and law enforcement agencies; outside the public sector only the occasional restraining influence of competitive pressures and unevenly applied regulatory statutes check such behavior. Because of this distinction,

[5] I thank Dorothy Guyot for suggesting this term.

[6] Compared to the United States, however, the statutes covering corruption in less developed nations are often *more* rigorous. Most developing nations not only have taken over western legal forms but have often adopted the most restrictive and demanding forms available. Whereas regulations governing public conduct in the United States make some allowance for political criteria—most notably in in the selection of postmasters—ex-British colonies are saddled with a set of laws that offer much less latitude in filling government posts. That is, the United States has institutionalized—legalized, if you will—practices which violate the law in many new nations.

[7] With the separation of ownership and operation in the modern corporation, stockholders are entitled to bring suit in such instances. "Corruption" in private business became an enormous problem in the west after the introduction of limited liability and remains significant today.

it follows that the larger is the relative size and scope of the public sector, the greater will be the proportion of certain acts that will meet our criteria of corruption. As the public sector is comparatively more important in most new states than in the west at a similar stage of development, this fact alone could be responsible for the appearance of more corruption in these nations. We must therefore make allowance for the effect of different economic systems when comparing the extent of corruption in different nations.

NEW NATIONS AND THE STUDY OF CORRUPTION

Recent speculation about corruption by social scientists is mostly centered in the growing body of literature devoted to the less developed nations.[8] It was clear, especially in the new nations of Africa and Asia, that the façade of politics was deceptive; the political party seemed to operate differently than its western counterpart and economic policy was made according to criteria that were difficult to fathom. In the context of this failure of nominally western institutions to function as anticipated, the search for explanatory factors turned increasingly to traditional social patterns and to more informal political arenas behind the façade.

Nor were these concerns confined to academic inquiry. Leaders of the new nations were frequently dismayed by the host of special pleadings they were asked to satisfy, by the behavior of their own party rank and file, and by the widening chasm between the policy decisions framed in the capital and what actually occurred at the village level. Plagued by these worries—and prodded, one must add, by press exposés and charges hurled by opposition parties in the parliament—special branches of the bureaucracy were created in many countries to investigate cases of corruption and to bring charges. The stream of official Commissions of Inquiry, a rivulet before 1955, became a veritable torrent by the end of the decade.

Corruption, which previously had been mentioned only with caution, now seemed to acquire the formidable power to bring down regimes, cripple administration, and sabotage economic growth. Spokesmen for the many new military regimes that have replaced civilian power-holders in Africa and Asia since the late 1950s never failed to cite corruption as a central reason for their seizure of power. Corruption was held responsible for the popular cynicism about politics, for stagnation or decline in per capita income, and for the reduction of national revenue. And the responsibility for growing corruption was laid at the door of the parliamentary system itself. The problem, as the generals saw it, was one of leadership; parliamentary democracy produced weak leaders serving at best a sectional interest and at worst a small coterie

[8] See, for example, Greenstone, 1966; Leys, 1965; McMullen, 1961; Myrdal, 1968, II, 937–958; Nye, 1967; Wertheim, 1965, Chap. 5; Wraith and Simpkins, 1963.

of mercenary followers. Such leaders could hardly command discipline or view policy matters from the national interest.

If the central problem was one of leadership, it is not at all clear whether *military* leadership was the appropriate remedy. Though the start made by military regimes was often vigorous and well-intentioned, the available evidence is not particularly reassuring. Army rulers in Burma (Ne Win), Egypt (Nasser), and Pakistan (Ayub Khan) in the late 1960s, despite uncorruptible leadership at the top, were plagued by corruption that, although it may not have attained the proportions it had in the previous civilian government, still constituted a severe obstacle to planning and administration. After modest short-run successes, military regimes appear to be almost as vulnerable to corruption as the regimes they replace.

The recent history of the new states thus demonstrates that we must seek the causes of corruption in factors of social structure and values that transcend questions of whether military or civilian personnel head the government. Since no state, old or new, is entirely free of corruption, the question is not its presence or absence. The relevant analytical problem is rather to determine how different political systems foster diverse levels and varieties of corruption and to assess the effects of corruption in that political system.

CORRUPT PRESSURES IN NEW NATIONS

Much of the analysis of corruption in Africa and Asia has concentrated on explaining why it occurs with some frequency in these nations. Leaving aside many superficial explanations that often betray both western prejudice and historical naïveté, the more serious interpretations emphasize either local beliefs and attitudes—i.e., values—or social and political arrangements—i.e., structure.

The accounts of corruption that focus on values often use the anthropological literature to show that much of what is considered corruption is in fact a continuation of traditional gift-giving practices. In the traditional context, the giving of a gift was obligatory in many circumstances and was embedded in an elaborate network of social alliances and status differences. Elites were often obliged, as patrons, to make gifts to their poorer clientele or to the community as a whole in a symbolic (and partly real) redistribution of wealth; those less well off were often expected to make token offerings to their patrons or leaders as a sign of their allegiance. The sense of obligation a gift created in the recipient made it an ideal means for building and maintaining a personal following and gifts were also important in repaying past favors or ending potentially bloody family or clan feuds.[9]

[9] For the classic analysis of gift-giving in traditional society, see Mauss, 1954. In a traditional society where fixed wealth is not very secure, gift-giving, far from being profligate, may be the wisest form of investment as it builds up credit which the investor may recall in the form of allies or goods and services at some later date—often with interest.

Practices had remained virtually the same, it was argued, and only the imposition of western forms had transformed traditional gift exchange into corruption. When the peasant who had been successful in court arrived with a basket of fruit for the judge's family, traditional patterns of gift-giving were clearly involved. The survival of such customary practices surely does account for the motives behind many petty acts of corruption, especially in rural areas. But it does not go far in explaining, say, a 10 percent rake-off on a contract for a new airport or much of the corruption in the modern sector of the economy. It is a partial explanation at best.

A second argument about the cause of corruption that focuses on community values emphasizes the importance of kinship ties and other parochial loyalties. The first obligation of a man in traditional society is to his close kin and then to lineage, clan, or ethnic group. Thus, when the brother of a personnel official asks his relative for a clerical post or when the cousin of a transport official asks for a taxi license, the strength of kinship bonds makes it difficult to refuse. A refusal would be seen as a betrayal of family loyalty. Traditional obligations to kin, tribe, village, or religious sect are so strong that they contribute to a certain amount of corruption in new nations.[10] Nepotism is a familiar form of corruption in the west as well, but the relative strength of kinship links, and the informal social sanctions that reinforce them, are more compelling in underdeveloped countries.

It is not just the strength of such parochial ties that creates many occasions for corruption, but rather their strength in relation to ties of loyalty to the nation. Although the citizen who asks an illegal favor from a relative in the civil service may be forgetting his responsibilities as a citizen, the civil servant in granting the request is acting against the norms of his public position. In all except the most traditional contexts he faces a conflict of values; on the one hand there are the public values of his government post and, on the other, the compelling obligations he owes to his family.

This conflict in values is often an unequal one. Western standards of official conduct are quite *formalistic* in the sense that they are relatively recent imports that are seldom held with strong personal conviction. They find minimal reinforcement in the indigenous social values of the host culture, and receive only half-hearted legal enforcement. Formal standards of public behavior in the new states have not been widely internalized and thus, in the absence of rigorous enforcement, behavior tends to be determined largely by the powerful parochial pressures at work in the local society. The gap between formal public norms and popular values is especially great in nations which were colonized by western powers, and it is this divergence

[10] These obligations have a semi-traditional variant in the "old school ties" that favored certain schools in recruitment to portions of the English civil service and in the "Ivy League" character of the American Foreign Service Corps and the Foreign Service Organization in the United States, especially prior to World War II.

which encourages corruption. Family and clan favoritism continue to have the sanction of tradition even though they are likely to run afoul of the modern bureaucratic standards which are formally in operation.

Loyalty to different values often implies loyalty to different groups or institutions that represent those values. In most traditional communities the plunder of outsiders was approved, even encouraged, while such behavior within the community was punished severely. Where, as in most new nations, loyalty to the nation-state is still tenuous, the individual feels little compunction to avoid acts that promote his personal or small-group interests at the expense of the state. A crucial question, then, is which institutions or groups command the effective loyalty of a citizen or public servant. It is not rare to find, for example, a civil servant who is at the same time an official of his tribal or clan association. As a civil servant he may take unwarranted liberties with state funds and place his incompetent friends in office, but in the tribal or clan organization he is a scrupulously honest guardian of the association's interest. The difference is simply that the clan or tribe engages his strong loyalties whereas the nation-state does not. To steal from the state burdens his conscience little or not at all; to steal from his clan or tribe would seem almost like stealing from his own family. "The ethic is there, but it has not yet been transferred from the seat of natural loyalty, which is the clan or tribe, to the new seat of loyalty which is the state" (Wraith and Simpkins, 1963, p. 50). Some new states have been more successful than others in promoting this transfer of values, but the strength of loyalty to the nation-state is still embryonic in most African and Asian countries.

The compelling nature of parochial ties together with traditional gift-giving practices thus account for a portion of the corruption found in underdeveloped nations. They represent, in fact, the sort of corruption one would expect to find in a country where essentially alien governmental forms and bureaucratic structures have been superimposed on a traditional order and have yet to take firm root. Such traditional motives, however, are of little use in accounting for the systematic extortion of bribes that occurs in some nations, or for what we might call "market corruption," which involves the selling of government goods and services to the highest bidder, whether he has "connections" or not. To understand these nontraditional forms of corruption we shall have to turn, not to values, but to structures.

Foremost among the structural factors that encourage corruption in new states is the tremendous relative importance of government in these nations as a source of goods, services, and employment. An appreciation of the pivotal role of the public sector in the less developed nations contrasts with the pattern in the United States and is essential to any account of corruption.

As an employer, the public sector in the new states of Africa and Asia represents the single most important source of status, wealth, prestige, and security. It is the dream of virtually every family to place at least one of its sons in the public service; the demand for western-style education is, in part, a by-product of this demand for public office. At a minimum, government employment offers a secure white-collar job of some power and prestige. The desirability of a secure job in a poor and often unstable nation can scarcely be overestimated. At best, government employment offers an unrivaled opportunity to improve one's status and prestige, to amass great wealth, and to exercise power with few restrictions. Small wonder, given these conditions, that the scramble for public jobs has sometimes assumed corrupt forms. The pressures for public employment are reflected in the rapid expansion of government bureaucracies in almost all new states after they gain independence—an expansion that usually goes well beyond that required by the assumption of new welfare and planning functions.[11]

This situation is not unlike that of England in the early seventeenth century, a period of "boom and scramble" when the price of public offices was continually rising due to increased demand. Office then, as now in less developed nations, was the major font of wealth and status mobility. Trevor-Roper (1962, pp. 10–11) has shown that of the 72 commoners elevated to the peerage between 1603 and 1629 (thereby doubling its size), the vast majority had made their money by holding office in the Crown's service rather than through trade or landholding. The sale of offices was legal at the time and the jockeying of Crown servants to make the necessary "connections" for their friends and relatives paid handsome rewards to those who met success. Selling government jobs is illegal in the new states but the posts themselves are every bit as valuable as in seventeenth-century England and every bit as avidly sought after. Here, too, the potential rewards of public office are great and there are few alternatives that can compete in attractiveness. The result is, barring rigorous enforcement of laws or a rare level of public spirit, that a good deal of corruption surrounds the selection, appointment, and promotion of civil servants.

Government in underdeveloped areas increasingly touches the lives of its citizens not only as an employer but as a regulator, producer, and consumer as well. The changing structure of government action since independence, as the new states assumed more responsibility for social welfare, economic planning, and actual production, has vastly enhanced the value of influence over political and administrative decisions. A typical Indian entrepreneur or trader, for example, must pick his way through a plethora of state and local regulations that are at best confusing and at worst contradictory. Given such conditions of great uncertainty, he is easily tempted to seek protection by using his connections and/or wealth. In doing so, he is

[11] Indonesia, for example, inherited an oversized 420,000-man bureaucracy which no cabinet succeeded in reducing, despite wishful policy statements to that effect. By the end of 1953 it had grown to a gargantuan 571,000 and continued to grow at a rate of "something like 10 percent per year" through 1957 and beyond. Cf. Feith, 1962, pp. 83, 306, 569. For estimates of the increase for other Southeast Asian nations, see Pye, 1967.

often dealing with politicians and administrators whose concern for public law is less than their desire for private gain.

The instruments of economic management in the new states necessarily have also given rise to a large variety of government-created privileges including import and export permits, franchises, limited licensing arrangements, and special protections for certain enterprises. Here the supply of valuable concessions is far exceeded by the demand, with the result that a corrupt "black market" develops which more closely reflects their actual value (Tilman, 1968, pp. 437–444).

A final structural change that has affected the extent of corruption is the expanding role of government as a producer and consumer, and as a taxer and spender. That corruption flourishes in such a situation merely reflects the fact that the possibilities for corruption are greater in a modern state where government actions touch more facets of its citizens' lives than in a traditional order where state activity is limited more to the functions of law and order, defense, and religious or ceremonial activities. Not only does the modern state directly employ a larger portion of its subjects than does a traditional polity, but a far larger share of the nation's income passes through the hands of government. Whether we measure by the number of people it employs, the number of functions it performs, or the amount of money it collects and spends, the activities of virtually every new state have expanded rapidly since independence. In the context of government expansion, some sections of the bureaucracy are more likely targets for corrupt influence than others. Accounts of corruption in the new states abound with instances from such branches of the public service as customs, public works, tender boards for government purchases and construction, licensing boards, excise and tax offices, loan agencies, foreign exchange control boards, and so forth. These all tend to be areas where the state dispenses valuable privileges or handles a great deal of money and where the nature of the task gives wide discretionary powers to those in authority. The traditional state performed these tasks, if at all, on a more modest scale, and thus the growing size and duties of the bureaucracy alone are likely to result in an increase in the total volume of corruption.[12]

When analyzing bureaucratic corruption in particular, there is another structural feature of many new nations that is of special note. Inasmuch as most colonial regimes were administrative states *par excellence*, they encouraged the growth of a large, skilled, elitist bureaucratic machine that dwarfed other power structures in the society. The growth of nationalist parties, especially in communist states, provided a competing structure, but

[12] This may occur even though the *rate* of corruption—as measured, say, by the proportion of all civil servants involved or the proportion of the national budget involved—may remain constant.

administrative structures were so firmly entrenched in most new states that they retained much of the *de facto* power, even if they were unable to exercise it collectively. What are the implications of such bureaucratic dominance? As Fred Riggs (1963) has shown, the relative weakness of political parties, business interests, trade unions, and other potential competitors has meant that the administrative apparatus is virtually uncontrolled, responsible only to itself, and thus free to pursue a policy of self-aggrandizement. No extrabureaucratic institution is strong enough to enforce either passive obedience to the political rulers or a service orientation toward the citizenry. In the absence of agencies that could enforce performance standards, bureaucratic factions blossom luxuriantly and each division of the apparatus becomes a virtual feudal domain that may parasitically exploit its clientele or the portion of the economy over which it wields power. Such chaotic patterns of corruption are often the hallmark of unchecked bureaucratic politics, as we shall see in the case of Indonesia under Guided Democracy.

There is still another sense in which bureaucratic dominance makes corruption easier. Many citizens in highly industrialized states are accustomed to dealing with civil servants whose status and education is not far out of line with their own. The situation in transitional nations is quite unlike this. Here the bureaucrat is a high school or university graduate who reads, say, French or English—the language of legislation—and who deals often with illiterate peasants for whom government, let alone its regulations, is a mystifying and dangerous thing. In approaching a civil servant, the peasant is not generally an informed citizen seeking a service to which he is entitled, but a subject seeking to appease a powerful man whose ways he cannot fathom; where the modern citizen might demand, he begs or flatters. In a survey of Philippine administrators, three-fourths agreed that "instead of expecting services or benefits as a matter of right, most citizens feel that they are asking a personal favor when they approach government officials for service or benefits" (Abueva, 1966, p. 25). That bureaucrats themselves encourage this attitude is equally evident from the fact that two-thirds felt that "instead of providing service or benefits as a matter of duty, most government officials feel they are doing these things as personal favors to citizens" (Abueva, 1966, p. 25). The huge gap of status, education, and information that separates civil servants and their clients in the less developed nations has at least two consequences for corruption. First, the administrator can make arbitrary decisions with impunity and can extort bribes and other special favors from his supine clientele. Second, the powerless client will more frequently offer a bribe in the hope of transforming the distant bureaucrat into a friendly patron and thus winning a favorable decision. If bureaucrats have particularly high status *vis-à-vis* their clients, then, and if there are no external power centers which could control the bureaucracy, corruption will normally thrive.

RESISTANCE TO CORRUPT INFLUENCE

Most of the values and structural features of less developed nations that we have explored are characteristics which *predispose* a political system to a high level of corruption. Traditional gift-giving practices and parochial ties make it more likely that forms of bribery will be attempted and that favoritism will be shown toward an individual's in-group. The great value of government jobs raises the probability that illegal means will be used to obtain them. The preeminence of the bureaucracy as a structure and the exalted status of the individual bureaucrat make it more difficult to restrain bureaucratic self-serving in general and the abuse of power by individual bureaucrats in particular.

These pressures toward corruption, while endemic in new states, are mediated by political institutions that either amplify or reduce them. Thus the extent of actual corruption depends heavily on the nature of these institutions. For a good test of how political institutions affect the level of corruption, we would want to compare two nations that were alike in all respects except for their political arrangements. No such perfect experimental case is available, but there is at least one instance that approximates such conditions. Both North and South Vietnam have much in common culturally and historically while their political systems are vastly different.[13] North Vietnam under the Lao Dong (communist) party has managed to minimize corruption while South Vietnam, even prior to massive foreign intervention, was characterized by widespread corruption.[14] In a more general sense, less developed nations which share many of the endemic pressures toward corruption have differed greatly in their actual levels of corruption; Tunisia and Singapore seem to have checked such pressures whereas Indonesia and Nigeria have been less successful. The crucial difference, I believe, is to be found in the nature of political authority and in the strength of certain political institutions and values.

Max Weber's analysis of how systems of political and economic order are created and maintained provides us with insight into how a society can effectively restrain certain forms of behavior and encourage others. A "convention" in Weber's terms—such as liberal democracy or merit administration—is a system of "order" which is largely guaranteed by the probability that deviation "will result in a relatively general and practically significant reaction of dis-

[13] North and South Korea might also qualify, but so little information is available on North Korea that a comparison is impossible.

[14] The accounts of corruption in South Vietnam are legion. The descriptions of administration in North Vietnam upon which this assessment is based include: Fall, 1956 and "North Vietnam: a Special Survey," *The China Quarterly*, No. 9 (January–March, 1962).

approval."[15] A system of "order" is thus supported by *social sanctions* and is to be differentiated from particular laws which are largely guaranteed by a system of enforcement that compels conformity by authoritatively punishing offenders. The modern administrative order that emphasizes faithful execution of public policy and enjoins private-regarding behavior must be underwritten, if it is to prevail, by both legal and social sanctions. For most underdeveloped countries, however, social sanctions militate *against* the modern administrative order and actually condone favoritism to in-groups, gift-giving, and other practices that directly undermine it. The modern administrative order must fight to survive in an environment in which sniping and sabotage by bureaucrats and citizens alike are quite in keeping with traditional customs. Deprived of social support, modern administration is forced to rely primarily on legal sanctions (a weak ally, lamed by unenforceable statutes and indifferent implementation) if it is to exist at all. Small wonder, then, that the new administrative practices fare poorly in most transitional countries; such practices imply values and attitudes to which their populations are not at all committed.

As with an economic or a political order, an administrative order thrives best if it is buttressed by social sanctions that reflect widely shared habits, attitudes, and values. The greater the strength and unanimity of the social sanctions that underwrite an administrative or political order, the more legitimacy we say that order enjoys. And, most important, the more legitimacy an administrative or political order is accorded, the greater the social pressures against acts that violate its norms.

How, then, can new administrative orders acquire legitimacy? Weber lists four possible ways. First, an order may be believed legitimate because it has existed for a long time—because it is traditional. As we have pointed out, this is hardly possible as a basis of legitimacy for a new administrative order in a society where tradation actually works against the new values. Another source of legitimacy can be "legality," a belief that what is legal is right. But, whereas the legality of the new administrative order may lead a portion of the westernized middle-class in new nations to support it, legality itself is of little significance among a citizenry for whom legality is synonymous with tradition, which, as we have just seen, works against the new order.

The two remaining ways by which an order may gain legitimacy, according to Weber, are either by an emotional belief in a newly revealed order, or by a rational belief in its absolute value. Here we find some key concepts for distinguishing between nations such as Tunisia and Singapore that have managed to establish a fairly legitimate administrative order and to control tendencies toward corruption and nations such as Nigeria and Indonesia that have experienced widespread corruption.

[15] This and the discussion of legitimacy which immediately follow draw heavily on Weber, 1947, pp. 127–130.

The emotional acceptance of a new order represents a symbolic commitment to its validity. For a new administrative order in particular, popular approval is largely dependent on an acceptance of the political order, for it is the administrative system that implements policies that emanate from the political order. Where the political order is perceived as illegitimate, the administrative order will be cast in an unfavorable light too; in the reverse case, where there is strong commitment to the political order, the administrative order, unless it is clearly identified as an opposition structure, will bask in its reflected glory.[16]

Historically, new bureaucratic norms often have acquired legitimacy by virtue of the fact that they were established on the heels of major political transformations that enjoyed wide support. Whether these transformations were liberal-democratic, nationalist, or communist in nature, they often helped legitimize a new administrative order in their wake. First, the new order was frequently viewed as the personal work of a single charismatic leader who by his blessing could confer legitimacy to any institution. Second, to the degree that the new political arrangements themselves achieve wide emotional acceptance, the political rulers are given a free hand to restructure the administration—to bring it into line with the new "legality." In this context one could compare the great capacity of a charismatic leader such as Ho Chi Minh and of a political structure such as the Viet Minh to legitimize a new administrative order in North Vietnam with the incapacity of Ngo Dinh Diem and his personal following to do the same in the South. A new political order can both institute an administrative order and generate the social sanctions to underwrite it.

The enduring legitimacy of a new administrative order depends largely on whether the transformation is sustained and institutionalized. Here is the factor which distinguishes the solid accomplishments of Bourguiba of Tunisia and Lee Kuan Yew of Singapore from the more transient achievements of Ghana's Nkrumah or Indonesia's Sukarno. In all four nations the triumph of nationalist movements provided the opportunity for large-scale administrative changes. But only in Tunisia and Singapore have these changes been put on firm footing by the creation of vigorous parties that have successfully inculcated new mass attitudes toward the civil service and that can insist on performance standards from the bureaucracy.[17] In Ghana, Indonesia, and

[16] In the early postindependence period, the bureaucratic order was often identified with the colonial regime, in contrast to the nationalist forces which had captured political power. Thus the belief in the new political order may have served to reduce the legitimacy of the still colonial-style bureaucracies in these nations. For a sensitive analysis of this situation, see Pye, 1962.

[17] Singapore and Tunisia both benefit also from a relative cultural homogeneity that facilitates wide acceptance of a new order and from their compact geography which simplifies the problem of control. Their institutional successes, however, remain the key factor.

other nations, the dominant party was more a personal following than an institution. Once the leader passed on or the revolutionary fervor subsided, the party was rent by rival personal cliques, party programs were sabotaged by personal strife, and corruption flourished with renewed vigor in an unrestrained or feudalized bureaucracy.

The rational acceptance of a new order, Weber's final route to legitimacy, is more important in the maintenance of a new administrative order than in its creation. In my view, the rational acceptance of a new political or administrative order over the long run rests primarily upon what political scientists would call the material "outputs" of that order—what it accomplishes in a more or less concrete way for the people who live under it. A rational commitment to a new order becomes especially significant when its charismatic or symbolic legitimacy begins to deteriorate at some point after its revolutionary establishment. If man does not live by bread alone, neither is a steady diet of ceremony and promises nourishing enough to sustain his faith in a political order. Social support for a modern administrative order, in all but the short run, depends on results—expanding opportunities for personal mobility, growing real income, greater personal security and employment opportunities, reduced inequalities in income, and so on. A bureaucratic system that is seen to have a hand in producing results of this kind will acquire a measure of rational legitimacy that will, in turn, create social sanctions for its maintenance. In this way, for example, Tunisia and Singapore supplemented their symbolic legitimacy with the legitimacy of effectiveness, thereby strengthening the new order; other regimes, often for reasons partly beyond their control (e.g., declines in world price for primary exports), were left with little *rational* legitimacy once the symbolic ties of the nationalist struggle loosened and jeopardized their survival.

Although conditions that encourage corruption are ubiquitous in most new nations, we have seen that these conditions can be contained and effectively managed. Legal restraints and vigorous enforcement play a small role and are overshadowed by the larger question of the legitimacy of the administrative and political order among key groups and in the population at large. A regime that enjoys both a symbolic and a rational commitment from its people and has effective institutions to channel these beliefs can bring to bear a variety of powerful social sanctions and new loyalty patterns to reinforce new administrative norms. A regime that must rely on the sanction of the law alone, by contrast, operates at a nearly fatal disadvantage.

CORRUPTION AS INFLUENCE

2

MEANS OF PERSUASION IN DIFFERENT POLITICAL SYSTEMS

Our central concern here is with the political significance of corrupt actions. Most acts we call corrupt are transactions in which one party exchanges wealth—or more durable assets such as kinship or friendship—for influence over the decisions of government. Whether the "buyer" seeks an honorary title (status), a post of some authority (power), or a large supply contract (wealth), the essential characteristics of the transaction fit this pattern.

Corruption may then be seen as just one of many ways a person can persuade someone who exercises public authority to act as he wishes—that is, as a kind of influence. Other sorts of influence, such as appealing to regulations, to ideology, or to equity, are quite legitimate means of persuasion so long as the power-holder acts within the rules. When we say that influence is corrupt we imply that without the special consideration of kinship, bribery, or friendship the public official could not have made the same decision.

Although not every corrupt act can be interpreted in this fashion, analyzing most forms of corruption in terms of a process of political influence allows us to examine corruption as part of a larger mosaic of political influence. This approach highlights the functional equivalence of a variety of acts of political influence—some of which violate all standards of community ethics and some of which are totally beyond reproach.

Were it not for the fact that a host of government decisions represent valuable commodities to some citizens, there would be little corruption. Nor would there be much corruption if the valuable things a state had at its disposal were simply sold at auction to the highest bidder. No modern government, however, sells civil service jobs or allots public health service and education only to those who can bid highest. Using the price system to allocate such services would violate shared standards of justice and equity. The problem, of course, is that demand for many government dispensations far outstrips their limited supply, and because the state makes no charge, or only a nominal one, the price for such services does not begin to reflect the supply-demand situation. In this context, the effort by many citizens to circumvent government non-price criteria for the award of these valuables takes the form of what one writer (Tilman, 1968) has aptly called a "black-market bureaucracy." Such attempts to influence government decisions are naturally more frequent where state activities are more pervasive. The legitimate influence of political pressure on legislatures, and ideological or ethical appeals compete against the illegitimate influence of wealth, kinship, and "connections."

Three instances of the use of wealth to sway state decisions will illustrate the expressly political perspective of viewing corruption as a form of influence. Each case exemplifies, in a different manner, what is likely to occur when wealth and power elites are separate. All are cases of influence, but in Thailand the political influence of wealth was achieved by corruption, in Japan by quite unexceptionable means, and in seventeenth- and eighteenth-century England by devices that are questionable but not illegal.

In England throughout the seventeenth and eighteenth centuries the lesser, wealthy gentry and the new commercial elite were able to buy positions of political authority either through the purchase of public office and peerages from the crown or, especially later, through the purchase of parliamentary boroughs. In this way, the new classes began to replace the older nobility in the affairs of state. Objections were raised to all these practices but they were not illegal until well into the nineteenth century.

In contemporary Thailand, by contrast, the business elite is largely Chinese, not Thai, and thus for ethnic reasons formal positions of authority are seldom open to them. Instead, members of the Chinese commercial community have established fairly stable relations with individual clique leaders in the Thai military and bureaucracy in order to protect and advance their entrepreneurial concerns. Many of the transactions that provide the cement for this informal coalition are quite illegal, but the relationships are, of course, enormously rewarding for members of the Thai bureaucratic elite who oversee the licensing and taxing of enterprises. Deprived of the privilege of outright office-holding, Chinese businessmen in Thailand have nevertheless managed quite well—albeit through corruption—to share quite fulsomely in the decisions which affect them.

Wealthy business elites in Japan, finally, operating in a very different fashion from Thai entrepreneurs, have also managed to wield great political influence. Working through the factions—particularly the "main current" faction of the Liberal Democratic Party (LDP) that has dominated elections in the postwar era—businessmen have provided the lion's share of this party's huge electoral war chest.[1] Rather than having each firm work out its own arrangements, as in the Thai case, Japanese businessmen functioned for a time collectively through an industrywide association that assessed member firms according to their assets and annual profits and passed on these funds to factions of the LDP. Japanese industrialists have thus had a large, and quite legal, hand in determining which clique would prevail within the LDP. The legislative program of the LDP has, of course, consistently reflected the support it has received from large business concerns.

These three illustrations are all cases in which wealth elites attempt, more or less successfully, to influence government actions. In the Thai case, much of what occurs meets the definition of corruption; the English case belongs in the category of "proto-corruption"; and the Japanese case would be difficult to construe as corruption in any sense. Using divergent strategies in each nation, wealth elites have achieved strikingly similar ends by bending government actions to their needs. The sale of office and parliamentary seats in Britain made the direct pursuit of office by the nouveau riche a common pattern. The ethnic background of wealth elites in Thailand severely

[1] See Soukup, 1963; in a comparable fashion, trade unions have contributed to left-wing parties.

circumscribe formal avenues to power and thereby promote more corrupt practices. But in Japan the existence of an organized party system allows businessmen to contribute openly and legally to the ruling party in order to gain their policy ends. Such factors as whether a nation has an electoral system, whether wealth elites are organized, whether there are ethnic or religious barriers that prevent wealth elites from formally holding office will thus partly determine the kind or amount of corruption in a political system. Each political system has distinctive routes by which wealth, as a political resource, influences government policies. The availability of some channels for influence and the exclusion of others set boundaries on the channels available to wealth elites for influencing formal power-holders, thereby affecting both the incidence and style of corruption.

INFLUENCE AT THE OUTPUT STAGE

Corruption, like other forms of political influence, often arises from the claims and demands people make on government. The study of how claims and demands are made on government in the industrialized west has for the most part focused on interest groups and the process by which such groups affect the content of legislation. If we distinguish between influence at the "input" stage (influence on lawmakers) and influence at the "output" stage (influence on enforcers after rules and laws have been promulgated), we can see that the "input" process has occupied the center of scholarly attention.

Students of politics in the new states of Asia and Africa, however have been struck by the relative weakness both of the interest structures that might organize demands and of institutionalized channels through which such demands, once organized, might be communicated to the political decision-makers. The open clash of organized interests, so common in the west, is often conspicuously absent during the formulation of policy and legislation in these nations. To conclude from this fact, however, that the public has little or no effect on the eventual "output" of government would be completely unwarranted. Between the passage of legislation and its actual implementation lies an entirely different political arena that, in spite of its informality and particularism, has great effect on the execution of policy.

Much of the expression of political interests in the new states has been disregarded simply because western scholars, accustomed to their own contemporary politics, have been looking in the wrong place. A large portion of individual demands, and even group demands, in developing nations reaches the political system, not before laws are passed, but rather at the enforcement stage.[2] Influence before legislation is passed often takes the form of "pres-

[2] It seems also that western scholars have perhaps underemphasized the importance of administrative politics in their own political systems, where both particularistic and organized interests can undo the effects of legislation or secure a favorable application of the law in their own case.

sure-group politics"; *influence at the enforcement stage often takes the form of "corruption" and has seldom been analyzed as the alternative means of interest articulation which in fact it is.*[3]

The peasants who avoid their land taxes by making a smaller and illegal contribution to the income of the assistant revenue officer are as surely influencing the outcome of government policy as if they formed a peasant union and agitated collectively for the reduction of land taxes. In a similar fashion, businessmen who protect their black-market sales by buying protection from the appropriate civil servants are changing the outcome of policy as effectively as if they had worked collectively through chambers of commerce for an end to government price controls. A strong case can be made that it may often be more "efficient" (and here the term "efficient" is used in the sense of minimizing the costs involved in attaining a given objective) to advance one's interests when policy is being implemented rather than when it is still being debated in the cabinet or in parliament. Three typical examples of situations in which corruption may help minimize costs for would-be influencers are suggested below.

1. Where the narrowness of loyalties or the scarcity of organizational skills inhibits the formation of political interest groups, the corruption of law enforcement may be the most efficient means of affecting changes in *de facto* policy.[4] The divisive loyalties of many peasants to their kinship, ethnic, village, religious, or caste groupings create social barriers that may preclude their organizing a common association that would advance their interests *qua* peasants. Given this fact, it is more efficient for the individual peasant to bribe local government officials, and thereby avoid the application of laws that may disadvantage him than for him to attempt to alter those laws.

2. Where legislative acts tend to be formalistic—where the administration of law is so loose and erratic that existing law bears little relationship to administrative behavior—it may be more efficient to make demands known at the enforcement stage than at the legislative stage. Even though interest groups exist, businessmen in developing nations may realize that the administration of even the most favorable tax laws will have little or no resemblance to what is called for in the statutes. That is, they may have to bribe as much to secure enforcement of a favorable law as to escape the provisions of an unfavorable one. Under the circumstances, then, it may make more sense for

[3] Although not all corruption occurs at the enforcement stage and not all "influence at the enforcement stage" is corrupt, the empirical referents of the two terms overlap considerably. A striking exception, of course, is the legitimate arena of "regulatory politics" in the west—an area that largely involves contending interpretations of statutes governing private-sector activity.

[4] Here we are assuming, of course, that there are few compunctions about corruption and few costs (e.g., probably of arrest) attached to such an act. Whether the bureaucrat "sells" influence—given a fixed reward—depends as well on the probability of his being caught, the penalty if caught, and his scruples.

each enterprise to quietly "buy" precisely what it needs in terms of enforcement or nonenforcement, rather than to finance an open campaign for a new law that would be as formalistic as the existing one.[5]

3. Where a minority is discriminated against and its political demands are regarded as illegitimate by the governing elite and the general population, its members may feel that open pressure-group action would expose them to attacks from more powerful groups. Therefore, they may turn to the corruption of politicians and/or civil servants in order to safeguard their interests. Throughout much of Southeast Asia and East Africa, a large portion of commerce and small industry is in the hands of Indian or Chinese minority groups which, even if they have managed to acquire local citizenship, are considered as aliens by most of the local population. It would be foolish, even suicidal, for these so-called "pariah" capitalists to seek influence openly as an organized pressure group. A healthy regard for their property and skin alike impels them to rely on payments and favors to strategically placed power-holders.[6]

Each of the three situations described, in which influence at the enforcement stage minimizes costs, are quite typical of the less developed nations.

The relative absence of organized interest-group activity in new nations is in part due to the fact that group loyalties are still centered at the family, village, or ethnic-group level. The peasant thinks of himself first a member of his extended family, then perhaps as a member of his village or tribal/ethnic group; he hardly ever sees himself as a peasant with interests similar to others who work the land. If he has political demands, they are not likely to be demands that embrace the entire peasantry, but instead will center either on his family's needs or on some small group to which he has direct links.

Implicit in this reasoning is the fundamental fact that the nature of most political demands in transitional nations is such that they are simply not amenable to the legislative process. Family-centered demands—e.g., a family's desire to secure a civil service post for its eldest son—are generally not expressible in legislative terms. When demands occasionally are made on behalf of wider groupings, they are likely to refer to ethnic, linguistic, or village units and only seldom can they be given general legislative form.[7] The prob-

[5] Occasionally politicians even may pass legislation that restricts the private sector so as to maintain the proper ideological stance while, at the same time, permitting private firms to operate unimpeded through corruption in which the politicians may share. Cf. Edelman, 1964.

[6] For a brief discussion of the East African pattern see Greenstone, 1966. For contrasting Southeast Asian patterns, Riggs, 1966, and Baterina, 1955, provide good descriptions of Thai and Filipino practices.

[7] "Pork-barrel" legislation catering to regional interests and legislation about languages of instruction in school or about local rule for minorities are exceptions to this statement. India has legislated preferential treatment for its *harijan* castes as has Malaysia for its Malay population.

lem thus lies less with the weakness *per se* of interest structures at the legislative stage than with the very character of loyalties in transitional nations and the kinds of demands fostered by such loyalty patterns. Couched, as it generally is, in universalistic language, legislation is often not a suitable vehicle for the expression of particularistic interests.[8] Influence at the enforcement level, on the other hand, is almost exclusively particularistic. It is scarcely surprising, then, that many of the narrow, parochial demands characteristic of new nations should make their weight felt when laws are being implemented rather than when they are being passed. Appropriate though it may be for organized groups in the modern sector, the modern legislative machinery of new nations is less effective in coping with the host of special pleadings coming from outside the modern sector.

The illustrations given above were, moreover, designed to show how potential political demands might be channeled along corrupt paths *even* in a functioning parliamentary system. For the majority of Afro-Asian nations, however, military rule has meant that interest group pressure on parliaments is no longer an alternative means of gaining political ends. In the absence of such open institutionalized procedures for influence, informal—often corrupt—channels have become all the more decisive.

Seen as a process of informal political influence, then, corruption might be expected to flourish most in a period when the formal political system, for whatever reasons, is unable to cope with the scale or the nature of the demands being made on it. Samuel Huntington (1968, pp. 59–71), in his analysis of what he calls "political decay" in the new states, views corruption from virtually the same vantage point. Rapid social mobilization—urbanization, politicization, etc.—he argues, has placed an impossible burden on the frail political institutions of new nations, thereby leading to the decline of political competition and to political instability, institutional decay, and corruption.[9] But corruption in this sense not only reflects the failure of the formal political system to meet demands from important sectors, but also represents a kind of subversive effort by a host of individuals and groups to bend the political system to their wishes. Those who feel that their essential interests are ignored or considered illegitimate in the formal political system will gravitate to the informal channel of influence represented by corruption. It is possible, as in the case of the American urban "machine," that while the formal political process may seem restrictive and rigid, corruption and other informal arrangements may add substantial openness and flexibility to

[8] There is a history of "special legislation" and, in England, "Private Member Bills" that attempted to meet particularistic demands or redress specific grievances at the legislative stage. The kinds of demands represented by this type of legislation have tended increasingly to shift to the administrative or judicial arenas.

[9] The frailty of such institutions is often due to the fact that they have been tailored to the demands and requirements of narrow oligarchies.

Table 2–1 Groups and Their Means of Access to the Political System in Less Developed Nations

Generally Easy Access to Formal Political System	*Groups Often Securing Access Primarily by Means of Corruption Because Denied Formal Access by Virtue of:*		
	Ideological Reasons	Parochial Reasons	Lack of Organization
1. Political elite	1. Indigenous commercial and industrial groups	1. Minority ethnic, religious, or linguistic groups	1. Unorganized peasants and other rural interests
2. Cadre and branches of ruling party	2. Foreign business interests		2. Unorganized urban lower classes
3. Civil servants' associations	3. Political opposition		
4. Professional associations			
5. Trade unions (especially those dominated by ruling party)			

ultimate policies. Thus important political interests that seem unrepresented in the formal structure may enter unobtrusively through the back door.

An empirical assessment of the interests served by state action would be inadequate, then, if it stopped at the content of laws or decrees and failed to ask in what direction and to what extent corruption altered the implementation of policy. Table 2–1 represents an effort to distinguish between those groups that usually achieve direct access to the formal political system in new nations and those groups that, for a variety of reasons, enter the competition for influence at a more informal level.

This rather sketchy composite cannot do complete justice to the situation in any single developing nation; it is, however, sufficiently descriptive of the situation in enough cases to alert one to the variety of interests that may seek to gain a surreptitious hearing. Aside from those groups that are blocked from formal participation for ideological reasons—for they are frequently in the modern sector and relatively well organized—the formal political system is *par excellence* the domain—virtually the monopoly—of the modern social sector. Minorities and the unorganized are placed at a distinct disadvantage since they face a formal political system that is simply not designed to accommodate them.

While a wide variety of groups may gain access to the political system through corruption, it is clearly those with substantial wealth who have the greatest capacity to bend government policy in their direction. Except for favors done from motives of kinship or friendship, it is the wealthy who are involved in most of the larger "deals" and whose influence is likely to overshadow that of smaller claimants. The reasons such powerful groups may operate corruptly rather than openly will be examined next.

PATTERNS OF ACCESS AND EXCLUSION

Any set of political arrangement creates its own distinct pattern of access and influence. When we call a given regime oligarchic or aristocratic we are essentially making a judgment about the size and nature of those groups in the society which exercise the most influence over public policy; we are describing a particular pattern of access.

The dominant forces in a political system usually have no reason to resort to corruption or revolution to make their influence felt, for the state is institutionalized to serve their purposes. If we look at local government in mid-nineteenth-century Prussia, for example, we find that government was tailored entirely to the needs and interests of local landed elites. Exploitation of the rural lower classes was built into the political system; "it was carried on legally and openly through preferential taxation and expenditure of public funds" (Anderson and Anderson, 1967, p. 160). Being virtually the owners of the state, landed elites had little reason to corrupt local officials.

Groups which may have engaged in bribery to advance their interests may cease to corrupt public officials once they have achieved greater formal access to power. Dutch business interests in colonial Indonesia follow this pattern (Wertheim, 1965, p. 122). Prior to 1920 they tended to bribe colonial administrators in Batavia to secure, on a piecemeal basis, the advantages they desired for their enterprises. Later, however, they became organized and their businesses became profitable enough to achieve many of their goals directly through legislation back in Holland. Thus, throughout the 1920s and 1930s there was no export duty on oil from Indonesia and little or no tax on rubber. The need for colonial financial interests to bribe agents of the state diminished in proportion as their open influence over the state increased.

The pattern of formal access to influence in any political system provides preferential treatment to some kinds of interests while slighting or even excluding others. Occasionally the excluded groups are without resources to back their claims (e.g., small, oppressed minorities such as Indians in the United States, aborigines in Australia) and cannot improve their position without powerful allies. More often, however, excluded groups possess political resources such as wealth, organization, numbers, or armed force that provide them with the potential for enhancing their influence. If the resources of the disadvantaged groups center around organization or armed force, they may well choose to engineer a revolution or coup that would refashion the political structure to give them greater formal power. If, on the other hand, the disadvantaged groups control wealth and property, they may seek an informal adjustment of their influence through corruption.

Broadly speaking, there are two situations in which important and powerful groups are likely to have less access to formal influence than one would anticipate on the basis of the resources they command. First is the common historical case of a pattern of formal access established in the past which has been gradually undermined by rapid social change that has yet to find formal expression in institutional changes or legislation. The formal rules, in this case, no longer reflect the new distribution of potential power in society. This situation was, of course, typical in much of Europe in the early industrial revolution when traditional aristocratic rule made little allowance for the new social forces then emerging. The second situation in which the gap between formal access and informal power potential is likely to be great is when there has been a *sudden political transformation* that diminishes or cuts off the access of groups that still command potent political resources. Recently independent nations with socialist ruling parties fall into this category, inasmuch as the new regime has often formally excluded such powerful groups as commercial and business elites and traditional chiefs and headmen who still command significant resources for influence.[10] The gap between formal access and potential for influence is thus widened both when the pace of social change outruns traditional political arrangements and when abrupt political changes suddenly displace groups that still have some weight to throw around. Excluded groups in both instances are a threat to the regime either by the violence of which they are capable—whether revolutionary or counterrevolutionary—or by their ability to corrupt the agents of the existing order.

To illustrate, we may compare the strains created by the gap between formal access and potential for influence in seventeenth-century England and in Ghana after independence. In the former case large landowning families and well-placed nobility enjoyed preferential access to positions of power and influence under the monarchy. The rapid pace of commercialization had even by this time, however, created a commercial elite of considerable wealth whose formal influence did not yet reflect their newly acquired power in the economy. As this new elite had interests that often clashed with those of the older landowning magnates, they employed their wealth to influence state policy informally. Some bought seats in Parliament by bribing small electorates or by advancing loans to impecunious notables who controlled a constituency. Others sought, by means of loaning money to the Crown, to assure

[10] Postrevolutionary France might fit this category too, inasmuch as the nobility was still a powerful force in the countryside despite the formal liquidation of the *ancien régime*.

themselves a lucrative franchise or a strategic post in the king's administration.[11] These activities were not illegal at the time, although older elites complained loudly against the steady infiltration of new men. The commercial elites were not, of course, the only excluded group since both the new urban mass and the increasingly destitute rural wage-laborers had no influence till late in the nineteenth century. But these latter groups had few resources and little organization with which to press their demands save by occasional riots that generally lacked both leadership and direction. Until they acquired the force of organization, their exclusion could be enforced without greatly threatening the system. Wealth elites, by contrast, had the resources to make their way informally to power.

In England at this time, then, we have an example of a formal political system that has not kept pace with momentous changes occurring in the society. A new wealth elite whose resource position is growing steadily more powerful has little formal influence while the older nobility, whose position has declined, still enjoys preferential access. The adjustment, to the extent one has been made, has not taken place formally but has occurred through informal, often corrupt means.

Ghana in 1960 presents a somewhat different situation in terms of formal and informal access. Nkrumah's Convention People's Party had become the dominant institution in structuring patterns of access and exclusion. The groups under the umbrella of the CPP that enjoyed preferential access to influence were the new, lower middle class of teachers, journalists, and government clerks, the so-called "veranda boys" representing the young urban unemployed who flocked to the CPP, party-dominated trade union leadership, a large number of petty traders, and, of course, the party branches. A number of other groups, many of which had enjoyed greater access to influence in the colonial order, were placed at a disadvantage under the new regime, although they were not without resources. Wealthy Ghanaian traders and large expatriate firms that dominated the export-import sector were foremost among the groups now largely excluded from formal access. In addition, many of the traditional leaders (particularly in Ashanti areas but elsewhere as well), some smaller, upcountry minority communities like the Tiv, and the older professional and bureaucratic elites were now relatively disadvantaged by the CPP.

The excluded groups each sought to improve its situation with the resources it had at hand. Many wealthy Ghanaian owners of construction firms and traders joined the CPP and contributed lavishly to its coffers and/or bribed administrators or politicians to acquire the needed licenses and permits and to win government contracts. For the expatriate firms the formal difficulties were somewhat greater since such businesses were in a legal sense outside the Ghanaian political system. But if their difficulties were greater,

[11] See, for example, Tawney, 1958, pp. 80–95.

so were their resources for illegal influence. Foreign firms doing business with Ghana quietly contributed 5–10 percent of their overpriced supply contracts to the CPP; they did a lucrative business and became the financial mainstay of the party.[12] Thus the interests of foreign business—and the CPP—were amply served by an informal system of highly priced corruption.

Other disadvantaged groups under the new regime—such as the Ashanti, Tiv, and the professional class—by and large lacked the resources to attain their ends corruptly. Consequently, the Ashanti and Tiv regions became hot beds of opposition activity and incipient revolt that became significant only when the military and the trade unions became alienated from the Nkrumah regime. Much of the professional class was also in opposition, but it lacked the broad following that made the Ashanti and Tiv a more palpable threat.

In Ghana during this period, then, we have an example of a new regime—a sudden political change—that has abruptly displaced groups that had enjoyed formal avenues to influence in the last years of the colonial regime. The formal pattern of access has, in a sense, shot ahead of the rate of social change, pushing aside groups that still have significant political resources. Those groups that control wealth or property have resorted to corruption to repair their position while those without wealth have turned to nonviolent or violent political opposition.

With the two examples of England and Ghana serving as guidelines, it is possible to construct a table that roughly delineates patterns of formal access and exclusion in some political structures and suggests the most likely consequences of nonaccess for certain groups. The nature of the disadvantaged groups in each case determines the kinds of pressures—corruption, violence, secession, coups—the regime will probably face.

The general descriptions in Table 2–2 require a fairly high level of generalization about types of regimes and therefore will not do complete justice to any particular historical instance. If such a schematization alerts us to the nature of groups denied open access in different regimes and the strategies they are likely, given their resources, to use in redressing their situation, it will have served its purpose.[13]

Among the groups classified as disadvantaged, I have included only those whose level of organization or potential resources allow them some means of remedial action. Thus, for example, although the urban poor were

[12] For a detailed account of these arrangements see the *Report of the Commission . . .*, 1966.

[13] The omission of a characterization of military regimes is by design. It seems, in my view, impossible to characterize such regimes as a whole. How, for example, could one possibly treat Burma under Ne Win, Egypt under Nasser, or Algeria under Boumedienne in the same category. Except for the favored access of the military and the common exclusion of precoup parties and autonomous mass organizations, each military regime is rather unique.

Table 2–2 Patterns of Formal Access and Nonaccess under Different Regimes and the Probable Consequences of Nonaccess

Regime Type	*Groups with Preferential Formal Access*	*Groups with Potential Political Resources Disadvantaged in Formal Access*	*Most Likely Means of Redress/ Reaction for Disadvantaged Groups*
1. Late feudal (and early absolutist) system (e.g., England, mid-seventeenth century)	Nobility, clergy, large landholders	New commercial and financial elite	Corruption (purchase of office, bribery)—and occasionally, opposition
2. Early Bourgeois Democracy with Restricted Suffrage (e.g., England, early nineteenth century)	Nobility, status elites, landowners, upper wealth elite	New worker and peasant organizations Moderate parties and new middle class	Strikes, riots, violence, revolutionary movements Opposition, reform
3. Urban "Machines" with Mass Suffrage (e.g., United States, early twentieth century)	Party stalwarts, lower-class electorate	Older status elite and new middle-class Business and commercial elites	Reform movements Corruption
4. Post-independence Socialist Regimes in New Nations (mass suffrage) (e.g., Ghana, 1960)	Party elite, party branches, lower-middle-class "official" mass organizations	Local and expatriate business elites Minority communities Professionals, old middle-class, traditional leaders Military	Corruption Opposition, secession Opposition Coups
5. Post-independence Conservative Regimes in New Nations (mass suffrage) (e.g., Malaysia, 1965)	Party elite, party branches, professionals, old middle-class business and wealth elites of dominant community	Mass organizations and peasant movements Minority and expatriate business groups Military	Riots, strikes, violence, revolutionary movements Corruption Coups

surely disadvantaged in seventeenth-century England, they are not mentioned because, except for largely futile outbreaks of rioting, they were without the organizational means to redress their situation. Later, however, when working-class organization took hold in the nineteenth century, they became a factor.

The groups a regime excludes from formal influence can tell us a good deal about some of the strains it will experience. To the degree that well organized and powerful wealth elites are shunted aside, large-scale corruption is likely unless draconian measures are taken to eliminate it or, failing that, to eliminate the wealth elite itself. Most regimes face corruption from wealth elites, but late feudal systems, urban machines, and regimes in new nations (socialist regimes because of the extent of exclusion, and conservative regimes because they often encourage a large private sector dominated by minority and expatriate wealth) face especially severe pressures. Regimes, on the other hand, that exclude primarily mass-based groups may experience less corruption but may be faced instead with civil disorder and revolutionary thrusts. In either case, when strong pressures for access are denied expression through existing institutional channels, the pressures pass into the "informal" political arena of corruption or violence.[14]

Underlying our argument about the problem of access is the assumption that excluded groups are unwilling to accept their lack of influence passively. One might imagine a feudal situation, for example, in which groups that are excluded seem to accept the legitimacy of their exclusion. But such cases are increasingly rare and, in most of the nations with which we are concerned, the existing arrangements are very much in question. Precisely how much in question is nonetheless an important distinction. Inasmuch as any regime is supported by certain values, beliefs, and interests, the use of more illicit avenues of influence, such as corruption and violence, will be increasingly resorted to as these supports cease to carry much legitimacy for a substantial portion of the society. Thus, as indicated earlier, the degree to which corruption and violence are employed to gain access bears an inverse relationship to the legitimacy of existing political institutions. The more political institutions are accepted as legitimate, the less likely it is that disadvantaged groups will resort to corruption and violence; the less existing arrangements are accepted as legitimate, the more likely it is that such groups will seek redress through unsanctioned means.

Much of what we consider as corruption is simply the "uninstitutionalized" influence of wealth in a political system (Key, 1936, p. 407). In most political orders, wealth occupies an uneasy position. Traditional regimes in

[14] The pressures toward corruption or revolution assume that influence over government decisions is an important goal for groups which are excluded. Such pressures are thus most relevant when the role of the state is more pervasive, and less relevant for, say, small subsistence agriculturists on the periphery of the state, who are happy to be left alone.

which positions of authority are allocated by status considerations, for example, make it necessary for wealth to beget status (e.g., by a favorable marriage or outright purchase of titles) before it can achieve power. Under a radical egalitarian regime there are few if any legitimate ways for wealth to buy power. The absence of legitimate avenues to influence in these instances increases the probability of corruption. In the modern liberal-democratic state, however, the pressures of corruption are somewhat diminished by the existence of more open avenues of political influence. The growth of large firms and business groups that may contribute to political parties, operate as pressure groups for legislation, and conduct expensive public relations campaigns lessens the need for bribery and other illegal techniques. Particular political parties, such as the Liberal Democratic Party in Japan, the Christian Democratic Party in West Germany, and the Republican Party in the United States, often come to be regarded as the main representatives of the wealthier strata. The decline of corruption is, in these instances, not a sign that the influence of wealth has been curtailed, but rather that it has been institutionalized and given a legitimate, not to say prominent, place within the political system.

Our feeling about corruption often depends on whether this "uninstitutionalized" influence of wealth is undermining a formal system of which we approve or disapprove. Thus, corruption in eighteenth and early nineteenth-century England seems less contemptible to us than modern corruption since it involves the subversion of an aristocratic or status-based monopoly of government. Corruption in modern liberal democratic or socialist regimes, on the other hand, seems especially damaging since it undermines both the egalitarian assumptions of majority rule and the principles of even distribution of civil and social rights of which we normally approve. Under liberal democratic regimes, corruption represents an additional and *illegal* advantage of wealthy interests over and above the *legal* advantages they ordinarily enjoy by virtue of large campaign contributions, muscle in the courts, and so forth. Wealth, in this sense, is doubly conservative in such regimes.

CORRUPTION AND VIOLENCE

Corruption and violence, as we have seen, are both means of settling conflicts between groups or individuals. As a strategy, of course, corruption is available only to those with connections and/or the wealth to purchase a favor. Nonetheless, for those who can manage it, corruption represents a more peaceful route to influence than force. Unlike violence, the corrupt transaction is also one in which the person is "influenced" receives some value from the person or group who does the influencing (Key, 1936, pp. 3–4).

In some historical contexts corruption has reduced the potential for violence either by providing a means for new groups to affect policy or by allowing ruling groups to "buy off" potentially violent opposition. After the Mexican revolutionary party (PRI) took command in 1911, it was faced with malcontented local military leaders whose potential for violence was great. By judicious use of political graft the ruling party managed to contain the situation and avoid a major outbreak of violence (Needler, 1961). The 1946 presidential election in the Philippines provides a similar instance of conflict management, but this time against left-wing forces. During that campaign the Liberal Party was temporarily able to beat back a growing potential for agrarian radicalism and violence thanks to the huge sums made available to it by the country's commercial elites (Baterina, March 1955, p. 81).[15] In England the growth of corruption has also been viewed as an alternative to violence by some historians: "For two hundred and fifty years before 1688, Englishmen had been killing each other to obtain power. . . . The settlements of 1660 and 1688 inaugurated the Age of Reason, and substituted a system of patronage, bribery, and corruption for the previous methods of blood-letting" (Wraith and Simkins, 1963, p. 60). Corruption and violence are both outside the law; corruption tends to be a peaceful but only temporary settlement of claims, whereas a physical confrontation is likely to be both more sanguinary and more definitive.

When economic wealth and political authority are in different hands within a system, corruption may firmly bind them together. In this fashion, corruption may serve as a stabilizing or conservative force that provides access to influence for a wealth elite that might otherwise finance opposition parties or even assist in violent attempts to overthrow the existing regime. This is simply another way of saying that those groups which successfully press their claims on a political system through corruption are, in the process, often wedded more firmly to that system. As Huntington (1968, p. 64) aptly expresses it:

> *Both corruption and violence are illegitimate means of making demands upon the system, but corruption is also an illegitimate means of satisfying those demands. Violence is more often a symbolic gesture of protest which goes unrequited and is not designed to be requited. He who corrupts a system's police officers is more likely to identify with the system than he who storms the system's police stations.*

Among those groups with a resource capacity for *both* violence and corruption, violence may indeed by symptomatic of a more extreme alienation from the political order. The fact remains, however, that for oppressed groups without the resources for corruption, the resort to violence is often the only strategy available.

[15] Preventing structural reform in rural areas may have bought temporary peace at the cost of greater long-term revolutionary pressures.

PROTO-CORRUPTION IN EARLY STUART ENGLAND

3

We have chosen early seventeenth-century England as one of two case studies of administrative, as opposed to electoral, corruption. In early Stuart England, as in contemporary Thailand, winning elections was less important as an avenue to power than currying favor with the ruler and his closest associates. It is this autocratic character of seventeenth-century British politics that makes it more suitable than, say, the parliamentary politics of Walpole in the eighteenth century, for comparison with military and other nonparliamentary regimes in the new nations.

The rationale for analytically grouping together cases where elections are not the decisive arena of political competition is based on the fact that this similarity in the institutional location of power is bound to entail similarities in the pattern of political influence. Conversely, changes in the one are likely to result in changes in the other. In this respect, the growth of dominant legislatures, political parties, and wide suffrage in the west meant a decisive shift in both the location of power and the pattern of influence. Those who had previously sought to ingratiate themselves with the king and his courtiers now cultivated the party boss and his lieutenants. Those who had capitalized on their connections or financial muscle to secure an administrative post now discovered that a seat in parliament might yield similar advantages. Those who had gained their ends by bribing civil servants found that bribing the appropriate politician, or—more legally—contributing to his campaign, would do just as well.

There are, then, certain common structural features of nonelectoral regimes that promote analogous forms of corruption. In particular, the dominance of executive and administrative agencies in such systems, the relative importance of a small circle of decision-makers among whom personal ties may be decisive, and the limited opportunities for public legislative influence contribute to the formation of distinctive patterns of corruption. Far from being an archaic pattern, the autocratic model of corruption has become increasingly applicable with the replacement of parliamentary forms by military regimes in the new states.

The choice of a pre-eighteenth-century European case immediately involves us, of course, in the difficulties posed by the legal conception of corruption at that time. Judged by modern standards, seventeenth-century England was a period of widespread corruption; the rapid pace of social and economic change had enlarged and enriched a commercial elite that was making its financial weight felt in the political system. At the time, however, many of the practices resorted to, including outright purchase of office, and letting of franchises to Crown favorites, did not violate existing legal norms.[1] What we are engaged in, then, is an analysis of proto-corruption—that is, of practices that are corrupt only by present-day standards—in order to see whether such practices serve much the same functions and produce similar consequences in early Stuart England and in a twentieth-century setting.

[1] One analytical advantage of the fact that such practices were not illegal is that meticulous records were often kept of favors and bribes, thus preserving much evidence that, in the twentieth century, would be destroyed.

THE PROPRIETARY STATE

Like most premodern agrarian states, England in the seventeenth century was a proprietary state. That is, the *state,* for all practical purposes, was a family—the reigning family—and the offices of the state were the *personal* property of the monarch to sell or dispose of as he wished. Until the proprietary theory was later undermined by new conceptions of national sovereignty, the state's administrators were the personal retainers of the king, crown lands were the king's lands, and state revenue was virtually the personal purse of the monarch.

Given the proprietary theory of the state, the major function of government in the seventeenth century was to act on behalf of the king as owner of the territorial state. The sharp distinction between actions of the king in his private capacity and in his public capacity did not really develop before the eighteenth century. Under the Stuarts as under the Tudors before them, England was virtually managed "as if it were a vast country estate belonging to the crown" (Bowen, 1963).

Despite the absolutist pretensions of Stuart kings, they never succeeded in appropriating all proprietary rights for themselves. First, they faced both a nobility and a financial elite bent on curbing the extension of centralized authority. Second, they had lost control of much of their own administration. The need for revenue resulted in the sale or the contracting out of many offices and duties, thus reducing the Crown's control over its would-be agents. The desire for allies among the nobility also led the Crown to confer offices to powerful nobles who could not be coerced into line without compromising the Crown politically. Finally, given the enormous difficulties in communication before the industrial revolution—as late as 1754 it took four days to travel the 175 miles from London to Manchester—a high degree of decentralization was unavoidable.

This curious amalgam of the Crown's continuing efforts to organize the state as an extension of its *personal* household, tempered by tendencies toward feudalization and the penetration of wealth elites, was reflected in the pattern of office-holding under the Crown. On the one hand, there were the servants of the Crown who had gained office entirely through the personal favor of the king or his family. Such officials, many of whom had professional skills, remained in office only so long as they remained in the monarch's good graces. On the other hand, those who had risen to office by virtue of their wealth or personal following were somewhat less dependent on the Crown; they often regarded their offices as freehold property that could not be confiscated. This group was ever sensitive to the Crown's efforts to limit the private prerogatives of office.

Regardless of how office was obtained in seventeenth-century England, no incumbent ever conceived of himself as a servant of that abstract entity known as the state, much less as a servant of the public. Some regarded themselves simply as personal servants of the monarch while others considered themselves the owners of valuable posts which they were free to use to their advantage. Neither conception begins to approximate modern norms of official loyalty to the state, let alone popular sovereignty. Particularly in England, where feudal and oligarchic patterns of recruitment persisted longer than in continental Europe, the notion of service to the Crown *as an institution,* rather than as a person, grew slowly.

Thus the traditional conception of office-holding prevailing in the seventeenth century led directly to practices we would now consider corrupt. Unlike the modern civil servant whose authority over subordinates is based largely on his skill, education, and seniority, and does not extend beyond office tasks, the seventeenth-century office-holder's authority was based more on his total status as a nobleman or a favorite of the Crown; his subordinates were quite likely to be *personal* retainers whose loyalty to him reached beyond office concerns. As his power was personal and as the powers and property attached to his office were his private domain, the seventeenth-century officeholder enjoyed a wide personal discretion unlike the narrow limits within which his twentieth-century counterpart operates. It was thus not thought unseemly for an official to sell off the subordinate offices in his department or give them to favorites, to speculate with the revenues he collected before passing them on, or to make a profit from the inside information he acquired.

It was this traditional fusion of personal property and office that provided such latitude of legitimate action to office-holders. Only by appreciating these traditional conceptions of office do the common patterns of seventeenth-century official behavior become intelligible. Much the same may be said for administrative behavior in less developed nations which, despite formal norms to the contrary, is influenced by more traditional notions of office-holding.

PATRONAGE AND CONTROL

POWER OF PATRONAGE

The power to confer and withdraw office is often the most significant means of political control exercised in the premodern autocratic state. England during the seventeenth century was no exception; the reward or sale of official posts, sinecures, titles, and pensions constituted the cement with which the monarchy bound together its allies and punished its enemies. By modern standards, the administrative apparatus was quite small, but in the context of a political world peopled by a narrow elite, it represented a supply of patronage and favor that weighed very heavily. The steady income a government post provided, the privileges and rights that the grant of an aristocratic title conferred, and especially the opportunities for both wealth and political mobility opened up by office-holding helped make Crown patronage a powerful political tool.

Most royal expenditures in the seventeenth century went to pay individual office-holders. One might even say that, aside from the judicial functions, the lucrative validation of status-based privileges, and foreign adventures, the Crown's administration was preoccupied with maintaining a vast army of household and executive servants which was the linchpin of its position in the realm. Under Charles I, the household staff alone—not including the judiciary, the military, or most revenue offices—was made up of over 1,800 people who consumed more than 40 percent of peacetime royal expenditure. The significance of the Crown as an employer can be seen from the fact that the income from the offices it awarded reached almost 10 percent of the total income received by the entire gentry class (Aylmer, 1961, pp. 27, 333).

The quest for office, title, and franchises and the spoils attached to them was the stuff of early Stuart politics. This is comprehensible only in the light of the fact that seventeenth-century politics is largely the politics of aristocratic factions and cliques rather than the politics of class and ideology. To be sure, class and religious issues existed and coalesced in the Civil War and the Glorious Revolution around the question of limits on the Crown's prerogatives. Such issues tended for the most part, however, to be subsidiary to the particularistic scramble of family-based cliques for the favor of the Crown. As late as the eighteenth or even nineteenth centuries, it is clear that English political parties were less significant political factors than were the shifting kaleidoscope of personal and territorial coalitions that determined allegiances.[2] Clique-based politics, important in the eighteenth century, was just as decisive in the seventeenth. Political competition was largely a narrow, intra-class affair of aristocratic cliques which managed to absorb many nouveaux riches each generation.

Except when the Crown's moves threatened the collective interests of the gentry or the growing commercial elite, its patronage was an effective political weapon. The fact that most power figures had personal-clientele followings rather than policy-oriented followings made it possible for the Crown to buy potential dissidents and secure potential friends by granting them office, the spoils of which could help maintain and reward their clientele. Similarly, the Crown's gifts or sales of monopoly and franchise privileges to big-time speculators served to cement ties between the monarchy and the

[2] Cf. Namier, 1961, *passim,* and Walcott, 1956, *passim.* Beer, 1965, places the transformation well into the nineteenth century.

London financial world. By the judicious deployment of its patronage the Crown thus endeavored to consolidate its political and financial position.

CONTROLLING PATRONAGE

The effectiveness of the patronage as a tool of political control depended on the Crown's being able to place individuals in office who were most amenable to its instruction. In this context seventeenth-century monarchs struggled continually to reverse the feudalization of the patronage and to increase their personal control over both appointments and administrative action.

The struggle to centralize the patronage in England was a part of a more general attempt by European monarchs with absolutist pretensions to restrict the accumulated prerogatives of their own nobility. The nobility, for its part, was wedded to an older system of spoils that "was sustained by aristocratic patronage, social heredity, amateurism, and, often, proprietary tenure." The Crown, on the other hand, hoped to replace this system with one "founded on centralized royal patronage, trained 'experts,' and discretionary appointments" (Rosenberg, 1958, p. 75). Establishing a merit system was not the Crown's goal, although it did wish to carry out its business with greater efficiency; the question was rather one of loyalty, with the Crown preferring servants dependent on royal favor who could therefore be more easily controlled. Only by creating its own personal servants and by reducing the independent power of nobles to appropriate offices for themselves and their heirs could the Crown place itself effectively at the helm of affairs.

The early Stuart monarchs, by comparison with their continental counterparts, were much less successful in centralizing the patronage. Family appointments and proprietary office-holding still predominated in much of the bureaucracy in spite of the Crown's attempts to centralize. Although the Crown made its own appointments for the major posts, most middle-level appointments were in practice made by superiors within the department, and a host of minor offices remained entirely outside the monarch's control. Stuart administration, then, represented a mixture of centralized patronage together with the survival of feudal and proprietary customs. Compared with the continent, it could still be called "the old-fashioned paradise of aristocratic spoilsmen in the West" (Rosenberg, 1958, pp. 104–105).

PERSONAL TIES AND PROTECTION

We will have grasped an essential feature of politics in England at this period (and in less developed nations today) if we understand that *personal ties* served to provide a level of personal security that is provided in modern industrial nations by law and established institutions. Such institutions lend a certain predictability to public behavior and provide a modicum of security. These guarantees were, however, largely absent in seventeenth-century England. There were no rules covering government appointments and promotions, tax and fee charges were subject to wide discretion, and the administration of justice fluctuated widely from location to location and case to case. In a context which thus lacked impersonal safeguards for one's wealth, job, or even physical security, individuals sought to protect themselves by building a network of *personal* alliances with well placed patrons.

We may call these alliances *patron-client relationships*.[3] In a patron-client alliance, the patron is more highly placed than the client and the bond between them is one of personal rather than group loyalty. Some positions lend themselves naturally to a patron role. The landowner commonly operates as the patron of his tenants (he may exploit them himself, but he does protect them from outside threats), the office-holder may function as a patron both of his subordinates and of those who need the services of his department, and any highly placed person is likely to become the patron of his relatives and friends.

A patron develops a following of clients by virtue of his unilateral control over resources the clients need. The major bases of patronage in seventeenth-century England were land and office. The predominant use of the former was by the large rural magnates who controlled their tenants and laborers. This form of patronage tended to be strong and durable as a landlord controlled his clients' very means of subsistence. Office-based patronage under the Crown, on the other hand, was much less durable as the patrons' resources (appointments, decisions, contracts) depended on his remaining in the favor of his superiors. The resources available to him might be much greater, but his hold on them was that much less secure.

THE CONTEXT OF PATRON-CLIENT TIES

Personal ties are, of course, influential in any political system. They are of greatest significance, however, when (1) personal security is precarious, (2) institutional/impersonal standards of procedure and behavior are formalistic or weakly developed; (3) political competition is largely confined to a narrow elite group, and (4) horizontal class or occupational interests are only weakly developed. These qualities are more or less characteristic of European states in the seventeenth and early eighteenth centuries and of some (but not all) less developed nations today.

The first two conditions are closely related to the problem of uncertainty. When traditional status-based rights have begun to erode but have

[3] For a detailed analysis of the operation of patron-client networks in underdeveloped nations, see Scott (1972, *in press*).

not yet been supplanted by a firm new institutional order, an individual's social environment lacks stability. This is reflected at one level in the limited capacity of the government to guarantee physical security or to enforce legal controls. At another level, property is insecure, not so much because the state is weak but because office-holders enjoy almost total discretion in the decisions they make. A businessman, for example, faces a host of tariffs, taxes, and licensing requirements that are subject to change according to the whim of the ruler or his minions.

A potential office-seeker faces an analogous situation. There are no set procedures or qualifications that govern entry to the administration; rather, the unpredictable ways of power-holders determine who shall achieve and retain office. Without the stable expectations and impersonal assurances of strong institutions, authority remains personal and thus subject to discretion and caprice. Protection and advancement in this context depend on the establishment of personal ties of loyalty with those who are in a position to do one the most harm or good.

The last two conditions under which the politics of personal ties flourishes are also closely related. When political competition is confined to a small elite stratum sharing basic interests in common (e.g., the exclusion of new participants, the protection of existing status-based privileges, etc.), the stage is set for a style of politics that centers on the struggle of different cliques for a larger share of the spoils. Little basis exists for policy cleavages within this elite. Those outside the charmed circle of participation can, in the short run, advance their interests only by attaching themselves to a patron who enjoys access to influence.[4] Gradually, of course, economic changes provided a basis for horizontal class and occupational ties which were fueled by policy and ideological differences. Before such ties develop, however, the political arena is occupied mainly by personalized clique structures which are united on the issue of preserving the elitist framework while competing mostly within it for private advantage. They do not depend on any policy-oriented constituency and thus they are irresponsible political units free to pursue the private advantage of their membership.

Conditions in England under the Stuarts were particularly conducive to the politics of personal ties. The literature describing this period indicates that patron-client groupings were the basic units of politics, and nowhere was patron-client politics as striking as in the competition for posts in the king's administration. Regardless of the social background of the applicant, patronage connections with important power figures were generally needed to acquire office—even for those with ability and wealth. Finding an influential patron was the first requirement for the office-seeker. A host of patrons then competed to place one of their personal clients in each promising open-

[4] The long-run alternative is, of course, to overthrow the system and/or broaden the basis of participation.

ing. Given the nontechnical character of much preindustrial administration, moreover, there were no obvious skill-based requirements for most offices; almost anyone could serve adequately. Choices among candidates were thus made largely according to the relative influence of their patron-brokers (Aylmer, 1961, p. 77).

The natural patron for many was a close relative by blood or marriage, while financial or friendship ties constituted the basis for other patron-client links. As the purpose of such links was mutual security and advantage, they fell into disuse when they were no longer profitable for both partners. The patron whose fortunes waxed lifted most of his clients in the process and acquired the resources to expand his clientele; the patron who waned jeopardized his clients' chances and found his clientele reduced as many sought more promising backers.

A description of patron-client links thus defines the structure of much political competition in early seventeenth-century English politics. Members of the office-seeking gentry worked through patrons at court, and the pattern which emerged was a network of "aristocratic clienteles which for so long formed the pattern of English politics" (Trevor-Roper, 1962, p. 27). This system, as we shall see, remained an important basis of English administrative and party politics throughout the eighteenth century.

Thus seventeenth-century English politics fostered a proliferation of practices we would now consider corrupt. Seeking offices for one's clients regardless of their qualifications was an integral part of the patron-client loyalties of the period. The purchase and sale of office, the exchange of favorable government decisions for cash or kind, the enrichment of family and friends from the Crown's coffers, and the abuse of less powerful or less well-connected citizens was typical of English government in this phase of its development.

ADMINISTRATION AND POLITICS

Patron-client networks within seventeenth-century English government were seen as political, not administrative units. Struggles among factions composed of allied patrons and their followers were political struggles. It would be some time before the English, following Prussian and French experiments, would attempt to insulate administration from politics.

The English citizen did not delude himself into imagining that he could appeal to a professional ethic of administrative service. He knew that, as a petitioner, he had either to work through a network of personal allies or, failing that, to offer some specific inducement or bribe to gain an official's sympathy. Appeals based on one's general rights as a citizen were doomed to failure. They failed because the official was not an administrator, in the modern sense, but rather a politician/broker for the narrow interests of his clients and his patronly allies. As a politician, the official had no constituency beyond his personal allies, and citizens recognized that his personal authority was scarcely subject to the discipline of evenly and equally applied standards. At this time in England's history, the bureaucracy was the central political arena for the narrow, opportunistic, clique-based structures that dominated the scene.

THE SALE OF OFFICE: WEALTH AND POWER

If the favoritism used to achieve office in the seventeenth century was corrupt by modern standards, on the other hand it had the sanction of representing time-honored traditions of aristocratic privilege. There were other widespread practices, however, that allowed wealth as well as status to be traded for positions of authority. Wealth was often combined with connections, but the growing role of marketplace criteria is evident in the selling or even auctioning of Crown offices, the contracting out of taxes and revenue collection, and the bidding for state-controlled monopolies and franchises. These proto-corrupt practices helped forge a *de facto* alliance between the monarchy and elements of the rising commercial elite. As the sale of office differs from the granting of monopolies and the subcontracting of state functions, we will treat the former in this section and the latter two in the following section.

THE PRACTICE

The sale of office was common throughout Europe during the seventeenth century. For the Crown, the sale of office was largely a way of raising revenue. For some purchasers an office represented a steady and relatively secure income (from fees and/or salary); for others it was an investment for profit; and for still others it was a stepping stone to another office of greater status or power.

Once bought, an office became a piece of personal property representing the state-enforced right to the fees, salary, and privileges attached to it. It was, then, a commodity; one that could be resold, traded, mortgaged, given as a dowry, or simply held for the income it produced. Owning an office might be compared to present-day speculation in government securities; some offices were more speculative, while others were "blue-chip" investments (sinecures, for example, with an assured income but no duties). The Crown also occasionally sold titles—such as peerages—either for revenue or to settle an outstanding debt. These titles were valuable not so much for the prestige attached to them as for the instrumental use to which the rights, privileges, and connections flowing from the title might be put. Titles conferred status, and in the seventeenth century, status was power.

Throughout much of Europe there grew up something resembling a "market" for offices. Offices were commonly sold in England at a price anywhere from three to four times their annual value to the holder. Since remuneration was often on a commission or fee basis, those posts relating to customs, taxation, and the like were more profitable in a buoyant economy and therefore fetched a higher price.[5] The scale of office-selling and hence its fiscal significance differed between nations and within one nation over time. It reached its most prodigious levels in seventeenth-century France, where a separate agency, *le Bureau des Parties Casuelles,* was established to handle the transactions. As a fiscal device, the sale of office was a success. Between 1610 and 1640 the proceeds realized from both the direct sale of office and the annual levies (*droit annuel* or *la Paulette*) that validated the holders' proprietary rights, amounted to between 25 and 40 percent of the known royal revenue.[6] The Stuart monarchy, by contrast, never became as dependent on the sale of office for revenue as the French Crown. This was partly a consequence of the relative strength of anti-absolutist forces in England as shown in the Civil War, which deprived the Crown of the power to appoint its own men to many posts. Another factor was simply the relative scale of the state apparatus; the French government was a much bigger operation altogether, both absolutely and proportionately, and the sale of office thus bulked more heavily in the state's revenue.

The Crown's desire to create new offices and step up sales as a financial expedient often makes it difficult to distinguish between a free-market sale and a mild form of extortion. Because the state itself was the seller of offices it could use political pressure to stimulate the rate of sales. Such pressures frequently persuaded wealthy merchants to purchase high offices and peerages. In this sense, the sale of offices and titles often represented a kind of forced loan to the state (in an era before government borrowing became institutionalized) exacted from the new commercial elite in return for the rights, privileges, and revenue the offices might provide.

SOCIAL MOBILITY AND THE SALE OF OFFICE

The sale of office provided an important avenue of social mobility for the growing bourgeoisie. The juxtaposition of a monarchy faced with pressing

[5] Swart, 1949, p. 34. Swart's book is still the best comparative study of the sale of office available. The market was far from "perfect" and varied with the applicant's social qualifications and his patron's standing. Aylmer, 1961, p. 219.

[6] Cf. Mousnier, 1945, p. 394. Mousnier has calculated that the sale of offices was much more important for revenue in this period than "le droit annuel." For the development of the sale of office in France, see also, Pagès, 1932.

revenue needs and an expanding, nonaristocratic middle class that was eager for the status and potential profit of office facilitated the political rise of the new commercial elite. As elsewhere in Europe, the sale of office led to a tacit alliance between the Crown and a portion of the national bourgeoisie (Rosenberg, 1958, p. 16).

Seeing that the rapid influx of wealth elites into middle and high offices was destroying what had been a quasi-feudal, aristocratic spoils system, spokesmen for the aristocracy complained bitterly about the preferment of wealth over merit (i.e., social background); they resented being shouldered aside by parvenues of "defective" origin. As has so often been the case, the effort to prohibit the marketing of office sailed under the banner of reform and anti-corruption. But behind the lofty arguments about what kind of administration best served the nation was also a struggle for power between the traditional status-based elite and a new wealth-based elite.

Throughout the seventeenth century the sale of office and related practices contributed to the stability of monarchical regimes by making room for ambitious members of the new bourgeoisie. This process was especially far-reaching in England, where it resulted not only from the purchase of office and title but also from the ease with which wealth elites could buy up rural estates and thus transform themselves into country gentlemen. This sort of class amalgamation softened somewhat the discontent generated among the merchant class, the lesser gentry, and genuine republicans over issues such as new taxes, forced loans, the creation of new Crown monopolies, centralization of patronage, and increased feudal dues.[7] While this did not prevent the Civil War, it did perhaps make it less bloody.

In France the amalgamation of wealth and nobility engendered by the sale of title and office on a large scale proceeded rapidly in the seventeenth century but ground to a halt in the eighteenth. For reasons that are beyond our concerns here, the *noblesse de robe*—that is, the ennobled bourgeoisie—gradually closed its ranks, making ennoblement increasingly less available as a channel of social mobility. (Swart, 1949, p. 122, and Rosenberg, 1958, p. 154). The cloture of this access route turned a good portion of the new bourgeoisie against the Ancien Régime, thus contributing to the role of the bourgeoisie in the French Revolution. This restriction of its access to status and power increased the likelihood that more radical means of redress would be sought. In England, by contrast, the permeability of aristocratic ranks throughout this period contributed to the long-run survival of the monarchy while transforming its policies.

[7] Cf. Taylor, 1960, especially Christopher Hill, "The English Revolution: A Marxist Interpretation."

OFFICE, REMUNERATION, AND CONTROL

The manner in which a person gained office and was remunerated had a great effect on the Crown's capacity to control its administration. The king's control was greatest over those office holders it directly appointed and provided with full salaries; its influence was tenuous indeed over officials who had inherited or purchased their posts and who were largely remunerated out of fees and gratuities.

The sale of office thus produced needed revenue but jeopardized the Crown's power. Once he bought an office, the purchaser had a lively interest in manipulating its powers and privileges to assure himself a regular profit. Many practices now considered corrupt were stimulated by the need to make the office a successful enterprise; subordinate offices were sold, bribes were extorted for services, and privileged information was sold for profit. When offices were sold to raise funds, moreover, the ability to pay became more important than the loyalty or qualifications of the official. Large-scale marketing of offices was, in effect, a sign that the Crown's need for revenue had taken precedence over the desire to ensure a thoroughly loyal cadre of officials.[8] Finally, many of the offices sold carried small salaries or stipends. Thus the cost of a short-run rise in revenue was that a large portion of the Crown's disbursements had to be set aside annually to meet its salary obligations to office holders. The fiscal device of selling offices thus tended to create an administration that was comparatively large, that was oriented more toward profit-making than service to the Crown, and that reduced the Crown's flexibility by consuming much of its annual revenue.

How an official was remunerated also affected his loyalties. Although he might receive a small salary and stipends for livery and board, he was generally expected to supplement his income by "living off the land." The fees, gratuities, and presents thus collected by officials, while corrupt by modern standards, were often routine in the seventeenth century.

The system of fees, gratuities, and presents insulated many administrators from central control. They were less dependent on the Crown financially and, hence, more independent—not to say rapacious—in their conduct. Entrepreneurial office holders tried constantly to raise the schedule of fees and gratuities to which they were entitled so as to increase both their annual income and the value of their office as a capital asset. The abuses of office that resulted were a constant source of anxiety to the Crown, although its capacity to rectify matters was severely limited. "Living off the land" meant, in

[8] The criteria of wealth and loyalty were often mixed, with loyalty of greater significance for the top posts and wealth for the middle and lower ones. It is thus a matter of relative emphasis. The system of salaried intendants in France represented an effort to restore central control over a bureaucracy packed with officials who had bought their posts.

effect, living off the lesser gentry, who were the main users of government services and who complained bitterly through their parliamentary spokesmen of the depredations of royal servants (Aylmer, 1961, p. 248).

Despite the decentralization and popular discontent it fostered, the fee and gratuity system had certain advantages for the Crown. It relieved the Crown from paying full salaries to its officials who, instead, collected much of their pay on a "piecework" basis from those needing government services. The system also avoided additional cash transfers at a time when each transfer meant a loss. Had the Crown insisted on the forwarding of fees to the Exchequer and then paid full salaries to its agents, a major share of its revenue would undoubtedly have disappeared. Finally, the system allowed the Crown to pass on some financial risks to its administrators; instead of the Crown's income fluctuating with the rate of fee collection, the income of the officials fluctuated. Given the inevitable difficulties in controlling and communicating with its agents in the seventeenth century, then, the fee and gratuity system was perhaps as efficient as any other. Like the sale of office, it was thus a consequence of the Crown's inability to control its administration. Limited power and revenue at the center plus a certain amount of *de facto* decentralization gave rise to a number of practices that were unavoidable and that, viewed from the standards of the twentieth century, would seem corrupt.

POLITICALLY ORIENTED CAPITALISM [9]

Politics in Stuart England can scarcely be understood without appreciating the proto-corrupt links that joined business and government. As we shall also see, the transactions between political elites and wealth elites in this period resemble current patterns of corruption in many underdeveloped nations and therefore assist us in analyzing these patterns.

Commercial wealth, as opposed to landed property, was greatly dependent in this period on the favor and protection of government. Business enterprises were subject to a host of state regulations, monopoly privileges, and arbitrary levies that could either bring about their ruin or ensure their success. This situation reflected the relative predominance of political power over economic power that typifies the preindustrial state. It was thus simpler, at this time, for a man of power to acquire wealth than for the man of wealth to acquire power. In order to thrive, a commercial venture either had to be directly run by well placed officials, or had to gain the support of administrators who could lobby on its behalf.

Our difficulty in appreciating the importance of politics to business in Stuart England—and in less developed nations, for that matter—arises from the modern capitalist assumption "that anyone who wishes to become an

[9] This term is borrowed from Weber, 1947, p. 280.

entrepreneur—to participate in the market—has free access to the system and full protection of 'property' and contract rights" (Riggs, 1964, p. 114). A safe enough assumption in twentieth-century capitalist economies, this was far from true in Stuart England. Because of the absence of a legal framework guaranteeing contractual obligations, the inability to predict tax loads or government regulation from year to year, and the uncertainty created by official discretionary power and a poorly developed market, a seventeenth-century enterprise operated under enormous risks.

To avoid extortion or confiscation in such risky circumstances a businessman generally needed official friends as well as commercial acumen. A successful commercial life depended less on the quality of the product or service offered than on the quality of the official patronage it enjoyed.

What is involved here is simply the need to buy "protection." Wherever landlords or businessmen are threatened by banditry or arbitrary officials, they will seek protection from any agency that can provide it. Should the state or its officials lack the power to guarantee security, private "protection armies," such as the Camorra or Mafia, are likely to fill the gap.[10] Where central authority is stronger, however, protection can generally be arranged through strategically placed officials who do a lucrative trade in bribes for their patronage.

Bribes for protection were not designed only to ensure that an enterprise would be left alone by the authorities. On the contrary, most of the attractive openings for profit in the seventeenth century were in the hands of the Crown; these included: the "farming out" of many taxation functions, such as the collection of customs on a rental basis; monopoly grants for the importation of wines, tobacco, tin, etc.; monopoly grants for the supply of salt, beer, etc.; exclusive patents for the manufacture of gold lace or for the operation of inns; government supply contracts for commodities or military equipment; and so forth. The hand of seventeenth-century government in the economy was ubiquitous, and access to any of these "guaranteed" sectors of the economy depended on winning the favor of the Crown or its principal agents. Ordinarily, nepotism and bribery were the essential tools with which access routes were carved. Commercial profit thus depended on political influence.

If we distinguish between *politically oriented capitalism* consisting of publicly guaranteed monopolies to do business or collect taxes and *market-oriented capitalism* based on the private sale of marketable commodities,

[10] In Southern Italy and Sicily, respectively, the Camorra and Mafia have done a thriving business in protection. The motives of their customers are apparent in the following quote from a Neapolitan businessman reported by Max Weber: ". . . the Camorra takes ten lira a month from me, but guarantees me security. The State might take ten times ten but would guarantee me nothing" (Weber, 1947, p. 311).

Stuart England was dominated by politically oriented capitalism.[11] The close association of business and government was encouraged and rationalized by doctrines of mercantilism that called for extensive government regulation and monopoly grants. While it protected much business activity, politically oriented capitalism had advantages for the Crown as well. The licences and monopoly grants awarded by the Crown provided a steady flow of revenue from commissions, fees, and special levies imposed on these enterprises.

More important still for the Crown's fiscal health were the rents derived from "farming out" revenue collecting functions to syndicates of businessmen and financiers who agreed to pay the Crown so much annually and keep the surplus receipts. The outstanding example of revenue farming in Stuart England was the Great Customs Farm that was awarded periodically to "patentees" from the elite of London's financial world. Since it supplied well over one third of the Crown's ordinary revenue, the Customs Farm represented the richest prize for entrepreneurs with connections (Aylmer, 1961, p. 64). Blocs of its shares could be bought and sold on the open market and a number of the patentees were regular paid officials of the Crown.

"Farming out" the customs duties proved so mutually advantageous for financiers and the Crown that it was not abolished until near the end of the century. For the speculators, who often bribed to get the patent, the Great Customs Farm provided a guaranteed profit and endless possibilities for lucrative deals with importers and exporters. For the Crown, the system not only ensured a predictable rental revenue and eliminated a large administrative burden but, above all, it gave the king access to the financial resources of the patentees. Without the short-term loans extorted from the patentees of the Great Farm, the spendthrift regimes of James I and Charles I could hardly have kept afloat.[12] Needless to say, the Crown's dependence on advances from the speculators in customs duties made it unlikely that it would complain about corrupt practices in customs administration. Having rented out much of the administration for fiscal purposes, the Crown thereby lost control over agents who were naturally determined to squeeze as much as possible from the kingdom's subjects.

The intricate web of monopolies, patents, licensing, and revenue farming spun by seventeenth-century monarchs helped create a capitalist class which thrived on the spoils and pickings of office, the collection of fees and taxes, and the favored sectors of the economy protected by monopoly and franchise privileges. Production for the open market, fraught with uncertainty and subject to extortion, was often less attractive than the guaranteed returns offered by a system of politically oriented capitalism. The system was less

[11] Eisenstadt, 1968, p. 153. The terms used by Weber to describe these types of capitalism are "irrational" and "rational."

[12] Tawney, 1958, p. 94. Tawney is here reporting the findings of Ashton, 1956.

like modern market capitalism and more like the "booty capitalism" of medieval Europe, a system in which speculators advanced funds for war in return for a share of the booty, or like colonial enterprises which operated with a monopoly charter and a captive labor force guaranteed by colonial authority.

Politically oriented capitalism, whatever particular form it takes, *involves the granting by the state of privileged opportunities for profit.* Such openings are available only to those with connections or to those who can pay for influence. The "capitalists," in these circumstances, are often officials inasmuch as state administrators are best placed to take advantage of the opportunities. Other "capitalists" must seek patronage or favor from top officials. They thrive according to the quality of their connections, their ability to bribe, and the extent to which the Crown is in fiscal need of the resources they can supply. Capitalists without connections, by contrast, have little chance of competing for the best prizes and are, moreover, subject to discrimination and extortion by officials that may jeopardize their business.

Given the modern conception of corruption as the misuse of public office for private gain, it is evident that the conduct of politically oriented capitalism depended directly on proto-corrupt practices. Most opportunities for profit-making depended on influence and bribes rather than on qualifications or merit. Even had capitalists wished to be left alone, they could not ignore the political conditions of their success. The Crown dispensed economic privileges, not by bureaucratic criteria, but by the need to win new allies and reward old ones or to buttress its flagging credit rating with London financiers. Practices that are today corrupt were an integral part of the mercantalist and revenue farming arrangements of the seventeenth century.

CONCLUSION

STRUCTURE

Having examined the structure of political administration in seventeenth-century England, we are in a position to summarize the basic patterns by which office was manipulated for private-regarding ends.

Three structural features of early Stuart England stand out in this context: (1) the size of the political elite and the context in which it exercises power; (2) the nature of cleavages within the elite; and (3) the relationship of wealth to power.

The political elite in the seventeenth century was a narrowly recruited group comprising the Crown, its principal courtiers, and the most powerful aristocratic families in the realm. Its power was drawn largely from Crown prerogatives and aristocratic privileges that were not dependent on popular approval for their exercise. Institutionally, the politics of this small elite found expression in the administrative rather than the legislative arena, making the administration something of a political coalition of Crown partisans. Parliament was concerned more with the limits of Crown power and less with performance standards within those limits. In its realm of power, then, the Crown and its agents were restrained only by their own broad, proprietary notions of political authority. Both the narrowness and the exalted position of the Crown's coalition permitted it to award posts on the basis of nepotism, to extort wealth from commercial elites, to make decisions on the basis of favoritism and bribery—and generally to misuse office for what today would be considered personal or political ends.

The nature of dispute within the elite also reflected the narrow, aristocratic foundation of elite recruitment. Except for the critical issues of the limits of monarchical power and religious freedom that sparked the Civil War, policy issues and ideological differencs were largely absent from the daily politics of the period. Instead, the competition of patron-client cliques for private advantage dominated. In the political arena formed by the Crown's administration, the ascent of a particular personal faction depended upon its gaining the monarch's personal favor and manipulating the patronage and prerogatives of offices controlled by clique leaders. The misuse of office for personal and clique advantage was thus not a simple matter of venality; it was, rather, an integral part of administrative politics among an aristocratic elite whose differences grew primarily out of the Hobbesian race for spoils and preferment.

A third feature of early Stuart England that fostered bribery and profit-seeking in administration was the rise of an affluent commerical elite that desired influence, protection, and status. Prior to the institutional protection afforded by the nineteenth-century liberal state, commercial profits depended on decisions of the Crown's ministers about matters such as tariffs, excise levies, and monopoly licensing. Security could be engineered only by a strategically placed patron in the administration who often expected favors or bribes for his services. The structural gap between wealth and power was thus bridged by transactions that would satisfy most twentieth-century definitions of corruption. Political elites used their control over the economy to engage in what amounted to an elaborate protection racket, the proceeds of which went to the Crown and into individual pockets. Commercial elites devoted a portion of their financial muscle to the purchase of opportunities in the privileged, government-sponsored sector of the economy.[13] The pattern of politically oriented capitalism that grew from this *de facto* alliance involved extortion on the one hand and bribery on the other.

In accounting for the private-regarding use of office we have emphasized structural factors such as the narrowness of the elite, the absence of institu-

[13] Increasingly in this period the "unconnected" commercial people who were excluded from many opportunities resented the "official capitalists" and found themselves on the side of republican sentiment.

Table 3–1 Classification of Corruption by Beneficiaries * and Degree of Marketization and Centralization

	Market (Price) Corruption	*Nonmarket Corruption*
Centralized	A (Crown and Commercial Elite) *Sale* (often in return for loans, credit) of office, monopolies, patents, franchises, and revenue farms *by the Crown.*	B (Crown, Commercial, and Aristocratic Elite) *Crown patronage* in high office, commercial privileges, and decisions *on behalf of favorites and allies.*
Decentralized	C (Commercial and Aristocratic Elite) *Sale* of office, monopolies, decisions, etc. by *individual officials.*	D (Aristocratic Cliques) *Aristocratic patronage* in high office, commercial privileges, and decisions, *among aristocratic cliques.*

* *Main beneficiaries are given in parentheses.*

tionalized responsibility, the personal character of intra-elite cleavage, and separation of political and economic elites. This is not to say that values were unimportant. The behavioral expression of proprietary, clique-serving values, however, depended on structural arrangements that facilitated and legitimized them rather than suppressed them.

BENEFICIARIES AND DEVELOPMENT

There was immense variety to seventeenth-century corruption. The outright auctioning of offices by the Crown contrasts with the gifts of office it arranged for friends and allies; the small private deals negotiated by the proprietary office holder for clique or family profit contrast with large tax-farming deals prepared by the Crown for fiscal purposes. Some order can be brought to this confusion by distinguishing between market and nonmarket corruption, centralized and decentralized corruption, and the beneficiaries of each combination. Table 3–1 is organized around these variables.

Not all the administrative practices we have described fall unambiguously into a single cell of Table 3–1. Many offices, for example, were sold only to friends or allies of the Crown, thus combining market and nonmarket criteria. The general trend under the early Stuarts, however, was from decentralized, nonmarket corruption to centralized, market corruption. As the table indicates, this shift reflected the growing alliance between the Crown and commercial interests and worked to the disadvantage of the independent aristocratic cliques that had previously controlled much of the patronage and spoils. The movement toward centralization and the price system in administration, apparent in England at this time, went much further in the absolutist regimes of continental Europe.

The evolution of administrative practices had notable consequences for social mobility, for political influence, and for central control. In terms of social mobility, the Crown's need of revenue and its desire for allies among the commercial elite provided many nouveaux riches with the opportunity to hold state office. Wealth became a path to office, thus undermining the traditional aristocracy's domination of the Crown's administration. Both mobility and the sale of economic privileges enhanced the political influence of the financial elites. The Crown and the financial elite were dependent on each other for revenue and protection respectively, with the result that the gap between wealth and power was spanned by a *de facto* alliance. Finally, the nature of the new alliance and the fiscal practices it entailed meant that the Crown still lacked control over much of its administration. Where aristocratic proprietary rights previously had limited its control, revenue farming and the purchase of office by wealth elites now created independent centers of power. Where the Crown had in the past found it difficult to restrain aristocratic office holders, it now found similar difficulties in restraining its newly acquired commercial allies.

CORRUPTION IN THAILAND 4

Despite the vast differences in culture and historical experience, corruption in contemporary Thailand is strikingly similar to proto-corruption in early Stuart England.[1] These similarities are not merely fortuitous; they depend instead upon important structural features shared by the two systems. In particular, early seventeenth-century England and present-day Thailand resemble one another in that: (1) political competition is (was) restricted to a narrow elite stratum in which many values are shared, (2) most intra-elite cleavages are based on personal clique struggles for power, wealth, and status rather than on policy issues or ideological concerns, and (3) potentially powerful wealth elites have relatively little *formal* access to political influence. The first two factors are related to the fact that both systems are more autocratic than electoral, while the gap between wealth and power is traceable to distinct historical factors in each system.

While forms of corruption in Thailand and seventeenth-century England are broadly comparable, specific forms and practices naturally vary a good deal. Thailand's administrative system, for example, bears the mark of her modernizing kings and princes of the late nineteenth and early twentieth centuries; entry into the civil service is by examination, administrative codes cover much official behavior, and most state employees are directly salaried. Modern administrative forms in Thailand also preclude the outright sale of office or the farming out of revenue functions as practiced in seventeenth-century England.[2] Such differences reflect Thailand's adoption of legal and administrative devices from the west, and we must look beyond such formal twentieth-century impedimenta to discover the broader similarities in the use of office and the exercise of informal power.

STRUCTURAL SIMILARITIES

NARROW SCOPE OF POLITICAL CONFLICT

Thai politics since the "revolution" of 1932, when the monarchy was shunted aside as the central ruling institution, has centered around the power struggles of small military-bureaucratic cliques. The limited "circulation" of elites that has occurred has followed on the heels of coups d'état confined largely to Bangkok and distinguished both by a narrow range of participation and by a lack of bloodshed. The scenario of these coups was so standardized as to have become virtually an institutionalized means by which rival military-civilian coalitions achieved power.

1 For the most part, my discussion of Thailand is drawn from literature based on research completed in the 1950s. Where more recent developments might affect the analysis, I have tried to indicate this.

2 Prior to the twentieth century, however, revenue farming was common practice in Thailand, officials were seldom salaried, and more traditional codes of official conduct prevailed.

Just as the military is the chief institution during transfers of power, the bureaucracy is the chief institution in the day-to-day exercise of power. Collaboration between the two is reflected in the fact that a majority of the members of ruling cabinets between 1932 and 1958 had bureaucratic backgrounds (Wilson, 1962, p. 155). The small thin stratum of about one thousand persons at the very apex of the Thai social pyramid from which cabinet members are characteristically drawn is no larger—and perhaps even smaller—than the comparable stratum from which the ruling elite was recruited in early Stuart England. Although this Thai elite is drawn from a wider social base than was the case in aristocratic England, the game of politics in both systems is nevertheless confined to a very small number of eligible players who have little to gain by cultivating a large following from the base of the social pyramid. The center of the political arena in England was occupied by a loose elite clique structure around the crown; the center of the political arena in Thailand is occupied by a comparable loose elite clique structure around the successful coup-group.

Thailand owes the narrowness of its political life largely to its having avoided direct colonial domination. The socially and economically traumatic consequences of colonial penetration that affected most underdeveloped nations have not been of sufficient scope or depth in Thailand to alter fundamentally the political process. Thus the peasantry, comprising 80 percent of the population, remains largely quiescent. It is composed largely of independent small holders rather than debt-ridden tenants, and it is not yet much affected by elite machinations in Bangkok. Both politically and commercially, Bangkok is tied to its rural hinterland only in a most tenuous way. As long as the relative security and adequate subsistance of peasants continues, elite politics in Bangkok can remain confined to that small sector of the population that is directly affected.

The political similarities between Thailand and early Stuart England hold up despite the fact that Thailand has some of the formal trappings of twentieth-century liberal democracy. Since 1932, for example, there has been a National Assembly. Except for brief periods, its main function has been to legitimize the existing elite's claim to rule. Until at least 1970 there were no real political parties to organize the competition and define issues. Many members of the Assembly were appointed, and government patronage and intimidation sufficed to keep most of them in line. Although Thailand also has secondary associations such as citizen groups and trade unions, most of these groups are personal creations of government officials and act as appendages to the clique structures in the administration (Riggs, 1966, p. 150). Thus the existence of an Assembly and secondary associations does not impede the domination of military-bureaucratic cliques.

The weakness of these institutions simply reflects the fact that there are no independent, cohesive centers of power outside the government that could provide a base of operations for them. The outcome of the clique struggles that dominate Thai politics depends overwhelmingly on control over key units of the military and the bureaucracy, with popular or parliamentary support counting for little. In such a nonelectoral system, the scope of political conflict is thus narrowed to that small elite stratum which commands the financial, administrative, and especially the coercive sinews of the state.

PERSONALISM AND FACTIONS: BUREAUCRATIC POLITICS

How is political competition structured within the narrow confines of the Thai political elite? As in England earlier, the unit of competition is the personal clique organized according to the patron-client model; these cliques are not motivated by policy or ideological differences, but are rather centered around a more or less amoral quest for power and spoils.[3] Few government actions can be understood without reference to "the foundation of political life in Thailand . . . the clique" (Wilson, 1962, p. 116; see also Riggs, 1962, p. 177). In Thailand as in England, the clique represents a kind of pyramiding of patron-client ties. Being an informal network of vertical, personal ties, a clique is particularly dependent on leadership for its stability. A schematic representation of a clique's structure is given in Figure 4–1.

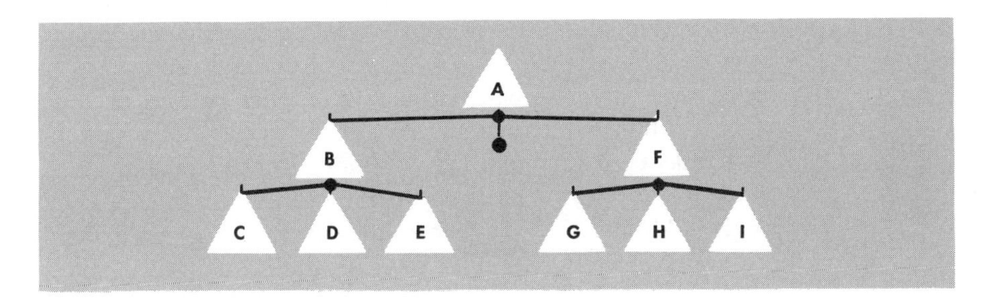

Figure 4–1 PATRON-CLIENT STRUCTURES

In Figure 4–1, patron *A* has two clients, *B* and *F*, who are in turn patrons of *C*, *D*, and *E*, and *G*, *H*, and *I* respectively. There are four features of the structure depicted here that distinguish it from more corporate organi-

[3] The amoral character of the competition is largely a function of the absence of extrabureaucratic agencies that could infuse wider purpose into government activities and enforce that pressure with sanctions. Limits to the competition are now largely set by nationalistic and traditional notions about the limits of self-seeking behavior, and by some long-run concern for maintaining the stability and legitimacy of present practices.

zations.[4] First, the ties involved are *vertical;* it is unlikely that *B* and *F*, for example, will be joined together by lateral ties of much strength, and the same is true for *C*, *D*, and *E*, and for *G*, *H*, and *I*. Second, because the ties are vertical, they tend to *span status differences*. Each of the patrons, major patron *A* and minor patrons *B* and *F*, are of higher status than their respective clients—it is in fact their higher status and access to rewards that allows them to function as patrons. Third, each direct tie represents a *face-to-face* relationship. This feature of clique organization places limits on the number of immediate clients any single individual can assemble; a leader can only expand the total size of his following by attracting subleaders who themselves control networks of sub-subleaders and their clienteles. As the network expands, the indirectness of the leader's control increases and the structure becomes more unwieldy. This brings us to the fourth feature of patron-client networks: their *dependence on leadership at each level*. Patron *A* is attached to clients *C* or *G* only through intermediate leaders *B* and *F*. In this sense, the network resembles a patchwork coalition in which *B* or *F*, as petty leaders, can switch to another patron and bring along their clients (who had no *direct* link to patron *A*). By the same token, the demise of any one leader often means the fragmentation of the entire network. If leader *A* should die, subleaders *B* and *F* may well go their separate ways, as they have no lateral ties. Thai clique networks are thus subject to a high degree of defection and fragmentation, which distinguishes them sharply from corporate groups such as trade unions or modern parties that have lateral ties or common interests which can better survive the vicissitudes of leadership.

The pervasiveness of patron-client structures in Thai politics may be traced to the same conditions which made such structures decisive in seventeenth-century England. As in England, the weakness of formal standards of procedure (e.g., selection, promotion) makes personal security contingent upon personal alliances. In addition, the fact that political competition is confined to a narrow, fairly homogeneous elite with few ideological or policy differences means that cleavage within the elite is more often determined by clique allegiances than by impersonal or categorical ties.

The personal bond between patron and client may spring from a variety of sources such as family ties, the personal links between military or bureaucratic superiors and their subordinates, the affection of students for their teacher, childhood friendships or school ties, or perhaps more utilitarian motives of mutual profit or gain. Regardless of the origin of the bond, the patron is expected to protect his clients and share his good fortune with them. The client must in turn support his patron in every way possible. The transactional nature of the relationship reflects the presumption of both partners that the bond should prove mutually advantageous. Based on the feudal

[4] I owe my general appreciation of patron-client structures to Carl Landé and his excellent paper "Networks and Groups in Southeast Asia" (1969).

model of older Siamese society, the motives of patrons and clients are an amalgam of mutual loyalty and the desire for gain.

The main basis of patronage in Thailand is government employment—either civil or military. There is no group of landed magnates, as there was in England, who could assemble large followings independent of the government. Maintaining a sizable clientele in Thailand thus depends on manipulating the powers of office. In particular, a strategically placed patron can influence the promotion and assignment of his followers, can provide them with financial opportunities through state enterprises, and can use his discretionary decision-making powers to attract new allies. The clientele of an upwardly mobile official is likely to expand at a rate commensurate with his growing capacity to distribute rewards. But a large clientele structure is particularly fragile since peripheral supporters have fewer ties of kinship or sentiment to bind them to the network than those at the core. All the large clique structures in Thai politics fit this pattern; they are cemented together mainly by the material incentives available to elite military and civilian officials, and they tend to disintegrate quickly if officials at the apex fall from office.

Beyond the all-too-human desire to become rich and reward friends, it is this clique structure of elite-based politics that promotes corruption and patterns it in certain ways. Within the ruling elite, cliques, as the units of political competition, are created, maintained, and expanded by manipulating the prerogatives of state offices in order to attract and hold powerful allies. Some of this manipulation stays within the bounds of legality; much of it, however, is distinctly corrupt. The distribution of high posts, financial opportunities, and government-controlled privileges represents the major stakes of political competition and also provides the adhesive agent for competing cliques (Wilson, 1962, p. 259). Corruption inevitably results when the political necessity of this distributive process clashes with formal regulations. Such corruption must be viewed, not as random greed, but as the consequence of a narrowly elitist political order that encourages clique conflict over the spoils of office—a conflict that is unchecked by any extrabureaucratic forces.

ADMINISTRATION AS POLITICS

The elitist, clique-based nature of the Thai ruling class has meant that "the fundamental questions of politics have revolved around political status—how shall the rewards of goods, prestige, and power be distributed within the ruling class" (Wilson, 1962, p. 165). This struggle is not joined in electoral contests or legislative battles, but in the civil and military administrative apparatus. As in early Stuart England, cliques serve as the "political parties" of an oligarchic order, in that they are alliance networks of office holders whose political arena is the bureaucracy. A cabinet minister thus becomes a clique leader with a constituency that is composed of his subordinates and other office holders with whom he has close personal ties. His success can be gauged by how well he protects and advances the particularistic interests of his clients. In this sense the transfer of a particular agency or function from one ministry to another, or a shift in relative shares of the administrative budget, signifies the outcome of a political struggle between cliques rather than an administrative decision designed to make the bureaucracy more efficient.

There is thus as much "politics" in Thailand as anywhere else. The difference is that most of it is located in administration (Riggs, 1966, p. 197). Whereas the legislature is often the main stage of politics in the industrialized west, with parties and interest groups as the main actors, in Thailand the bureaucracy is the stage of politics and cliques are the main actors.

The many anomalies of Thai administration are cast in a new light once we understand that, because the bureaucratic elite is the political elite, much of administration must be seen as politics. This perspective, suggested by Riggs (1966, Chap. X), helps explain why a bureaucrat's influence and connections are more decisive for his success than his administrative skills or his technical competence. It also helps explain why loyalty is more highly rewarded than the ability to make technically "correct" decisions, and why, especially at higher echelons, merit or seniority criteria are less influential for career success than the quality of one's personal alliance network. In a political arena it is scarcely surprising that power, influence, connections, and political loyalty should take precedence over administrative skill, training, and experience. Or, to put it differently, there are no basic structural distinctions that would lead us to expect a markedly different pattern of politics and corruption in Thailand than in early Stuart England.

As each alliance network seeks control of key posts, promotion and job assignments become a part of the clique struggle for political ascendancy. The process of budget allocation is political test of each clique's ability to extend its empire at the expense of its competitors. Development programs or government enterprises are calculated more to augment the funds and patronage of a clique than to raise national productivity. Even seemingly routine administrative decisions that are fraught with political consequences for competing cliques may become the objects of power struggles.

Such political intrusions into Thai administration often take corrupt forms. Recognizing that such corruption has political meaning helps us move beyond explanations which focus exclusively upon mere opportunism or traditional family loyalties. In Thailand, as in early Stuart England, administrative corruption cannot be understood apart from the political system that structures it and infuses it with meaning.

CORRUPTION IN THAILAND

Many of the particular forms of proto-corruption typical of early seventeenth-century England do not occur in Thailand. State offices are not sold to the highest bidder, nor is there a traditional aristocracy that has a feudal, hereditary claim to certain posts.

Furthermore, the Thai government no longer relies on profit-seeking syndicates for the collection of state revenue.

In spite of these differences, which can be traced to Siam's adoption of modern administrative forms, the pattern of political administration in both systems is remarkably similar. First, the intrusion of clique-based favoritism and patronage into administration is characterstic of both systems. For Thailand, this intrusion is more likely to occur in questions of promotion and job assignment than in questions of entry into the governing circles, but this does not alter the fact that personal political connections make or break administrative careers in both systems. Secondly, office holders in the two systems share a more or less personal conception of their authority—a conception that contributes to the exploitation of official powers for private gain. A third similarity concerns the use of state enterprises and government regulatory powers (licensing, monopoly grants, and so forth) in both cases to serve the ends of clique patronage or private gain. Finally, a system of politically oriented capitalism is as typical of twentieth-century Thailand as it was of early seventeenth-century England. By examining the main forms of corruption in Thailand, the links between political structure and administrative practice will become apparent.

CLIQUE FRAGMENTATION AND CORRUPTION

The basic building blocks of a clique are personal ties between individuals. For an ambitious Thai military or civilian official, the problem is how to assemble a loyal and well-placed clientele that will protect him and extend his influence. In piecing together a following larger than merely his closest friends, moreover, the official competes against other potential patrons attempting to mobilize clienteles of their own. Unless the patron is so powerful that he overshadows his rivals, he must offer competitive *tangible inducements* to attract new followers.[5] Here is where corruption enters, since these inducements may take the form of political promotions, opportunities for profits, or the promise of such benefits. Although many rewards (e.g., promotions, assignments, etc.) can be granted within the law, others violate even the relatively permissive Thai legal order. Thus the diversion of public funds, mismanagement of state enterprises, and kickbacks from government contracts are a natural part of clique-building.

[5] Here it is important to specify that clique structures in Thailand (except for the Chinese) seem to depend on *positive* inducements. That is, the rules of seniority and the security of bureaucratic tenure are firm enough so that officials who choose to avoid political affiliations will not thereby jeopardize their employment, although they will limit their chances for moving up. I suspect that in seventeenth-century England personal alliances were as necessary to avoid loss of office as to enhance one's upward mobility.

Because it is pyramided far beyond the confines of kinship and lifelong friendships, a great many links in a large clique structure are heavily dependent on the mutual advantages they provide. The pressure for corruption comes from the top as well as from the bottom. On the one hand, clients expect, as a reward for their loyalty, that they will be shown favor in promotions, that they will be granted financially rewarding assignments, and that their benefactors will wink at a client's manipulation of office for profit. On the other hand, the patron must supply benefits to allies which cannot be granted directly; he must therefore prevail on his clients (and on their subordinates) to use their own offices so as to distribute favors, contracts, and other concessions that will help solidify the clique network. He thereby not only tolerates corruption among his clients but actually promotes it.

A potential coup-group is brought into being with a series of promises concerning who will get what, if and when the group makes it to power. The major participants in this dangerous adventure expect to be compensated for the risks they take with powerful posts and some influence over the distribution of enterprises, contracts, and monopoly concessions controlled by the government (cf. Silcock and Evers, 1967, p. 96). Should the coup succeed, the ruling clique must also forge links with enough key bureaucrats, military leaders, and businessmen to solidify its control and ward off possible challenges. Since the ruling clique must offer concessions to its new allies, the process of ruling group solidification promotes a kind of feudalization of the administration, with each clique leader presiding over his own bureaucratic domain. So long as a powerful ally remains loyal to the ruling clique, he is given virtually free reign in managing the affairs of his own administrative sector. An agency head is thus at liberty to favor his own clients within his agency, to let contracts to his business allies outside government, and to become a director of private enterprises whose profits are affected by agency decisions. To speak of clique politics in Thailand is thus, in the same breath, to speak of corruption.

PERSONAL AUTHORITY AND PERSONAL FAVORITISM

As a political arena, the Thai bureaucracy is highly *personalistic*. As in seventeenth-century England—or, for that matter, contemporary Spain, Italy, and many Latin American nations—it is impossible to discuss the high incidence of nepotism and personal favoritism in Thai administration without reference to the personal nature of authority relationships.

The influence of a particular Thai official is not simply a function of how high his post is in the formal organization of government. His standing depends just as heavily upon the quality of his personal connections with other power-holders and the strength (not just numerical) of his own clientele. Thus behind the formal system of bureaucratic ranks lies an equally elaborate but informal system of personal status that often serves to undermine formal authority. Like the seventeenth-century office holder in England, a Thai administrator tends to view many of his subordinates as personal retainers who owe him a personal loyalty beyond mere bureaucratic norms. He tends to view the powers and property associated with his office as part of his personal domain—a domain to be used in the pursuit of private and/or clique gain (Golay *et al.*, 1969, p. 285). The higher the post an official occupies, and the more secure his connections in the elite, the more easily he may violate regulations when it suits him. Lower officials, by the same token, understand that formal regulations are residual, in the sense that they may be contravened on the personal authority of a superior.

The formal rules of the Thai bureaucracy are thus inadequate as a guide to the actual behavior of officials, for they ignore the personal links that determine what superiors may expect of subordinates and vice versa (Siffin, 1966, pp. 161–162). By virtue of such personal bonds, moreover, the rules are invoked in a sporadic and particularistic fashion; the official may apply them or not, depending on whether it is in his interest to do so. Standards of performance do exist, but they are essentially political rather than administrative. Thus an official does not evaluate his subordinates' performance by how efficiently they do their work, by how closely they adhere to regulations, or by their technical virtuosity. He is instead likely to value them according to how loyal they are to him personally, how effectively they advance his interests and those of his allies, and how useful their own network of personal contacts may be to him. The fact that a superior will tolerate many violations (often corrupt) of administrative regulations among his subordinates, whereas he will strike with dispatch against any junior official who shows personal disloyalty to him, is indicative of the relative weakness of administrative as opposed to political norms.

The expressly personal and political basis of authority in Thai administration leads to many practices that border on the corrupt. This is particularly evident in the selection among candidates for promotion or choice assignments. In practice, the outcome of the competition is contingent on the influence exercised by each candidate's patronly allies. The best connected may also be the best qualified, but he is just as likely to be the least qualified. "Within the service, career advancement generally requires the *personal support* of superiors or the political leverage of influential relatives or friends" (Shor, 1962, p. 34). As an official ascends the bureaucratic ladder, of course, the controlling effect of his personal alliances on his future is magnified.

An ambitious young official, knowing that advancement hinges on personal ties, seeks to become the protégé (client) of a high-level patron—often a relative or family friend. In return for personal loyalty and service, the protégé expects to be shown favor over nonclients and to share in the good fortune of his protector. The political decisiveness of such ties is recognized by the Civil Service Commission. First, the Commission implicitly recognizes the rights of agency heads to rule their personal domains and therefore avoids any interference in day-to-day personnel management. Secondly, instances of appointment, promotion, and discipline where major clique political interests are involved are recognized as political matters and are settled more as questions of power than as questions of correct procedure.

The Thai bureaucracy, allowing for exam-based entry requirements and a certain degree of administrative routinization at lower levels, is thus highly politicized to the patronage needs of Thai clique structure. A portion of those patronage needs can be fulfilled without violating the existing regulations. Just as often, however, such transfers and promotions involve breaching legal restrictions by appointing well-connected candidates without the required qualifications, by illegally transferring personnel, by overlooking absenteeism, by using subordinates for personal business, and so forth.

It has been common to regard the personal quality of authority and the corruption associated with it as a vestigal remains of traditional Thai norms. This interpretation has some justification inasmuch as the distinction between personal and official roles is rarely a sharp one in traditional settings. What seems more important in the Thai context, however, is the fact that the political structure of the state has both facilitated and reinforced the role of personal ties. If the elite were more broadly based, if extrabureaucratic agencies were more powerful, or if a mass electorate controlled the choice of the top elite, the demands for certain policies and standards of performance would become difficult to resist. As it is, the small military-civilian elite has no need to be responsive to an unmobilized peasantry, a packed parliament, or a thoroughly domesticated commercial class. A given political order may either encourage or discourage a personalistic patron-client style of politics; the Thai political order, with its narrow distribution of power and its "management" of parliament and civilian associations, serves to prolong the dominance of personal, clique-based cleavages.

PETTY CORRUPTION

Petty corruption is quite common among lower-ranking officers. Typical instances include the common gifts given regularly to clerks to expedite one's case, bribes (often extorted) to avoid prosecution for minor offenses, kickbacks in the hiring of labor, violations of regulations in response to an official/patron's request, and so forth. Although each transaction involves a relatively small sum, the cumulative total adds appreciably to the income of petty officials. Informal gratuities are exacted in some areas of administration with such uniformity that they could be considered as institutionalized fees—except that the proceeds accrue not to the government but to personal income. Clearly, the "pettiness" of corruption refers only to the size of each transaction and not to its total impact on government income or policy.

In assessing petty corruption it is important to distinguish between "speed" payments and "distortive" payments, and between extortion and bribery. "Speed" payments generally involve bribes that *expedite* a decision without changing it, whereas "distortive" payments change the decision and contravene formal government policy. Paying a clerk to issue a driver's license quickly is a "speed" payment;[6] paying a clerk to issue a license to someone who is not legally entitled to it is a "distortive" payment. Although both varieties of corruption occur throughout the Thai bureaucracy, it is safe to say that most speed payments occur at lower administrative levels while distortive payments are more common at middle and higher levels.

Distinguishing between bribery and extortion is more difficult. We commonly speak of extortion when an official demands an illegal payment and backs up that demand with a threat to punish, whereas bribery refers to the use of more positive inducements. A Thai factory inspector who seeks out building code violations and demands money from the owner in return for not prosecuting is practicing extortion. A factory owner who offers cash to an official to help secure an import license is practicing bribery. Extortion is more common in such administrative activities as law enforcement, taxation, and inspection where penalties are involved; bribery is more common in licensing, government procurement, contract awards, and loan agencies where important services and privileges are dispensed.

At least three related factors encourage this *petty* corruption. In order of ascending importance they are: low income, personal authority, and the absence of control structures.

It is now virtually dogma among administrative reformers to cite the low income of civil servants as an incentive to corruption. As far as it goes, this explanation has some validity for Thailand. There has, in fact, been a decline in civil servants' real income since World War II, and public sector salaries are substantially below private sector rates. Despite the security, status, and occasional bonuses he can count upon, the government servant feels his income does not match his "socially expected costs of living." "The quest for ways to augment their real income has therefore become a fundamental preoccupation among Siamese bureaucrats" (Riggs, 1966, p. 249). Some officials take part-time positions to supplement their salaries, but for many the easiest course is to raise their income by illegally manipulating the powers of their offices. The important question, however, is why petty corruption is such an easy option for Thai bureaucrats.

In part, the answer lies in the personal conception of office and the great chasm of power and status that separates the official from his public.

[6] When "speed money" is collected uniformly from all applicants for a given service, the term is less appropriate. In that case, the payment becomes merely a toll charge which does not expedite—except in the negative sense that, if it is not paid, the application will probably be "lost." If speed money ("dash," "bakshish") is accepted from only a few, it is mildly distortive in that the payer's case is considered out of turn.

When his decision assists someone, a Thai official expects that it will be viewed as a personal favor and not simply as the impersonal product of regulations. Since Thai citizens understand that the rules are formalistic, on their part they are *personally* grateful to whomever seems directly responsible for a decision which benefits them. Operating under these assumptions, a member of the public who does not already have a connection with the official who can assist his case sees a gift (solicited or not) as one means of creating the necessary link—of enlisting the personal support of a powerful man. Furthermore, we should recall that "the public" we speak of consists often of Chinese who, as aliens, are not presumed to have any rights, and of uneducated Thais to whom law is a capricious mystery and for whom deference is the only possible strategy. Those who can are expected to somehow reward the official who serves them and those without means must show respect. "In no case is a demand for one's rights likely to produce the desired response from an official" (Siffin, 1966, pp. 212–218). Quite apart from low salaries, then, the exalted position of the official *vis-à-vis* his public and the fact that claimants usually seek *personal* rather than group benefits contribute to a high level of petty corruption. No one is so foolish as to assume that he may put his faith in laws and regulations; one's standing in law is of less consequence than one's personal connections.

The manipulation of public office for private gain is either facilitated or discouraged by the political environment in which a bureaucracy operates. A cohesive, policy-oriented ruling party, for example, can create a system of sanctions and rewards that serves to discipline the performance of the bureaucracy. In this respect, the fragmentation of the Thai administration into personal clique networks is facilitated by the weakness of extrabureaucratic controls. Since 1932 neither the military, which has the power but not the cohesion, nor the political parties, which lack both, has been able to bring the bureaucracy into line. Bureaucratic self-indulgence therefore remains unchecked—even encouraged—at both the top and bottom of the administration. At the top, corruption is more often related to political ambition; at the bottom, it is more often motivated by the undiluted desire for monetary gain. Although the misappropriation of *government* funds is dealt with severely, "the gentle extraction of funds *from the public*—so long as this is done discretely and not by overt coercion—is likely to be tolerated" (Siffin, 1966, p. 218; emphasis added). The patron-client style of administration and the corruption that it fosters are, in the final analysis, made possible by the absence of any institutions that could impose countervailing standards.

GOVERNMENT ENTERPRISES: BUREAUCRATIC CAPITALISM

In Thailand and in most underdeveloped nations, as in seventeenth-century England, wealth that is unsecured by political protection is tenuous indeed.

The impersonal guarantees of property and contract rights that undergird modern market systems are absent. Given this situation, it is axiomatic that officials with political power are able to manipulate that power in a way that maximizes their own wealth.[7] The translation of power into wealth may occur in either of two ways. First, politicians and bureaucrats may enter business directly—in public or private firms—and take direct advantage of legal monopolies, state subsidies or quotas, and government contracts to amass private fortunes. Although the term has been used somewhat differently by others, I would call such individuals "bureaucratic capitalists." Alternatively, politicians and bureaucrats may simply exploit an existing commercial elite by systematically extorting benefits from it and "selling protection." I would call such individuals "bureaucratic extortionists," with the understanding that they are primarily squeezing the commercial elite rather than the general population. This distinction is an analytical one, inasmuch as a particular official can, and often does, take advantage of both roles. Patterns of bureaucratic capitalism are analyzed in this section, and bureaucratic extortion of the private sector in the next.

State enterprises have a long history in Thailand. Although the pace of nationalization and new ventures quickened in the 1950s under Field Marshal Phibun, this represented more an extension of past policy than a new departure. Irrigation and electric power had long been state functions, just as whiskey distilling, tobacco production, and playing-card manufacture were government monopolies. Since 1945 the government acquired holdings in cement, batteries, glass, tin, and textiles and has come to dominate in the production of sugar, paper, gunny bags, and timber (Insor, 1963, p. 155; International Bank for Reconstruction and Development, 1959, pp. 90–91).

The precise pattern of government involvement in public enterprise is difficult to gauge since it is not fully disclosed in public documents. Each enterprise is affiliated with a particular ministry; some were wholly owned and operated by the ministry, others were controlled by it but not directly or wholly owned, while still others were only partly financed by the government. The ministry of Industry, for example, had a hand in forty-seven enterprises in the mid-1950s. The ministries of Interior, Agriculture, Finance, and Defense were also heavily involved in public or quasi-public enterprises.[8]

What is the political significance of this huge network of governmental

[7] This is, of course, a matter of degree, since power can be used to generate wealth in any political system. What we are suggesting is that power is much more easily translatable into wealth where impersonal guarantees for property are largely absent.

[8] Riggs, 1966, p. 305. Riggs gives no indication of the size of each enterprise. Silcock (1967, Appendix A, pp. 308–316) offers a list that distinguishes the degree of ministry control in each instance. The following examples from Silcock's compilation show the wide range of government-controlled undertakings: Prime Minister's Office—Yanhee Electricity Authority, Thai Television Co. Ltd.; Ministry of Industry—Gunny Bag Factory, three sugar factories, two paper mills,

commercial ventures? In a limited way the growth of public enterprise has conformed to nationalist stirrings among a portion of the elite. Because the domination of the private sector by local Chinese is often resented by this group, nationalization and Thaification represented synonymous goals that could find expression through the expansion of the state's role as a producer. Beyond whatever popular appeal government enterprise had, it is clear that, at the same time, it served more prosaic—if not more important—ends for the Thai elite. Those ends are perhaps most obvious in the context of the general failure of such enterprises as profitable or efficient ventures. As the International Bank survey of government undertakings stated:

> *All of the state industries, except the monopolies, have proved unprofitable by commercial standards. . . .*
>
> *The enterprises were too often initiated by persons with political influence who had no special knowledge of the industry or particular concern about ultimate success. . . .*
>
> *Both assets and liabilities are swollen by loans to and borrowings from other government agencies—a pernicious system which not only makes the balance sheets unintelligible but is obviously open to abuse [International Bank . . ., 1959, pp. 92–94; cited in Riggs, 1966, p. 209].*

What is involved, behind the cautious tone of the Bank's report, is the use of government enterprises for the patronage needs and private income of those at the top of the Thai political clique structure. The potential revenue yield for the government was definitely a minor consideration next to the large payroll that could be distributed to clique clientele and the possibilities for the misappropriation of loans and subsidies afforded these enterprises.

In the postwar era most ministries within the Thai bureaucracy have, by using their revolving funds, become centers of commercial activity. This activity often bears little relation to the ministries' formal purpose. Virtually all the higher posts in public enterprises, which paid comparatively lucrative salaries, were filled on the basis of clique patronage considerations. The funds of these firms, as World Bank reports and the revelations following Field Marshal Phibun's fall in 1957 indicate, were illegally manipulated for personal or clique gain. What we have, then, is a system of public enterprise which served narrow political ends, both legally and illegally.

Wickerwork Factory; Ministry of Interior—Metropolitan and Provincial Electricity Authorities, five pawnshops, Poultry Organization, Market Organization; Ministry of Agriculture—Cold Storage Industry Organization, Rubber Estate Organization, Thai Plywood Co., Ltd., three banks; Ministry of Defense—Fuel Oil Organization, War Veterans' Organization; Weaving Organization, two refineries, Bangkok Dock Co. Ltd.

As a vehicle for personal and clique advantage, public enterprise was a success. Being outside the normal bureaucratic structure, these undertakings were subject to few of the restrictions governing regular administration and could therefore be manipulated in relative safety. There is every indication, in fact, that the growth of public ventures under Phibun was explicitly seen as a way of adding to the legal financial opportunities of clique supporters. Even with the legal freedom provided by this device, the history of public enterprises is checkered not only with annual deficits, overstaffing, and poor business practices generally, but also with outright corruption in the form of misappropriation of funds, fraud in accounts, unsecured personal loans, and so forth. One of the more glaring examples of such corruption during Phibun's administration was the National Economic Development Co. Ltd. (NEDCOL) established in 1954 under the Ministry of Finance. Its ostensible purpose was to operate as a holding company for a number of sugar and gunny bag factories. In practice, it was closely affiliated with the clique of General Phao (Director General of Police) and used to provide income and patronage to clique supporters. Following the 1957 coup in which Phibun and General Phao were ousted by Field Marshall Sarit, it was discovered that less than half of the government grants to NEDCOL had been invested in its subsidiaries; the bulk of the funds had simply disappeared. What had been a dismal failure in economic terms had been a political and financial asset of major importance for Phao's clique.

Most public enterprises were controlled by one or another of the major cliques. The composition of the board of directors of a particular venture is a reliable indicator of its clique affiliation. Banks, for example, can be distinguished by clique affiliation; data from the mid-1950s show that the Bank of Asia, managed by Sarit's half-brother, and the Union Bank of Bangkok were dominated by the Sarit clique, while the Bank of Ayudhya and the Bangkok Bank were in the hands of General Phao.[9] After the 1957 coup the Bangkok Bank came for a time under the wing of General (and Minister of the Interior) Prapas' group and the Bank of Ayudhya was chaired by the Director General of Police. Each bank was instrumental in providing credits to clique supporters, in assisting favored business, and in giving jobs to clique members. Top officials, for their part, were in a position to assist affiliated banks with government deposits and other financial privileges.[10]

[9] These examples are taken from T. H. Silcock, "Money and Banking," in Silcock, 1967, pp. 183–185.

[10] It should be added that in a few official enterprises, perhaps because of their key importance for the Thai economy and its international reputation, clique representation was precisely balanced. These included Thai Airways, the Provincial Bank, and the Thai Rice Co. (Riggs, 1966, p. 302). Here is an example, then, of clique collaboration that places limits on competition and corruption to ensure the survival of the clique system as a whole.

From the record, it is obvious that the productivity and the profitability of public enterprises was not a preoccupation of the elite. The staffing, accounting procedures, and investments surrounding such ventures reveal little concern for such goals. While some viewed national enterprises as a way of reducing Chinese economic power, in actual practice many national enterprises were managed by Sino-Thai businessmen who were connected with the appropriate clique while other Chinese firms benefited from contracts negotiated with public companies. One must thus conclude from their actual activities that Thai public companies were largely the vehicles for clique competition and aggrandizement. The prevalence of general corruption, mismanagement, huge deficits, and incompetent personnel that typify their operation are emphatically not simply the result of poor planning or a lack of skills; they are, rather, part and parcel of the political uses to which they were put by a narrow, clique-based elite.

The highwater mark for the political exploitation of public enterprises occurred under Phibun. His successor, Sarit, relied more on the private sector to reward his supporters and liquidated many national enterprises. These enterprises had, after all, become something of a national scandal and the corruption they engendered began to threaten the availability of international loans.[11] Although I have no data, it would seem likely, given our interpretation of these enterprises, that the new government would have liquidated especially those firms controlled by *rival* cliques.

BUREAUCRATIC EXTORTION OF PARIAH CAPITAL

The predominant role of the Chinese in Thailand's commercial activity extends back as far as the seventeenth century when Thai kings granted them noble titles and appointed them to key posts in state monopolies and trading ventures. In the twentieth century the Chinese elite has come to dominate the import-export trade, rice milling, shipping, banking, and much of the large-scale retail trade. Through language-group associations, trade organizations, and interlocking directorates, this commercial empire is controlled by a small elite that deals directly with Thai political leadership.

As in seventeenth-century England, wealth is insecure in Thailand. What distinguishes the Thai case from the English case, however, is the fact that the commercial class is recruited from an alien community and cannot aspire to formal positions of authority in the political system. Since the reign of King Wachirawut (1910–1925), the clamor for a reduction of Chinese control over Thai economic life has become an essential part of nationalist sentiment. Although the pressures on the Chinese community have waxed

[11] The mismanagement of some monopolies, such as Prapas' pork monopoly had also begun to work some real hardships on the population. The slaughtering fee added to the producer's costs while the price of pork for consumers already was artificially high, thus creating some resentment of nationalized enterprises.

and waned with the vagaries of domestic and international politics, the balance of power has clearly been with the Thai elite. The task of the Chinese elite is basically the defensive one of minimizing the pressures for expropriation and assimilation that threaten their wealth and community leadership.

In the context of Chinese political weakness, the possibilities for extortion were enormous. In the early 1950s Chinese businessmen and small traders were harassed constantly by police raids, revocation of leases or deeds, new control measures, or sudden inspections. The immense tangle of laws and decrees made it unlikely that any business could avoid running afoul of the law. "In these circumstances bribery, squeeze, and the payoff have become common features of business functioning in Thailand." [12] While those businessmen without connections who resisted being importuned were likely to be raided, have their property confiscated, or be placed under arrest, a business could avoid prosecution by paying off the appropriate officials. This pattern of corruption, we should add, applies to much of the rest of Southeast Asia and East Africa, where politically weak alien commercial elites are compelled to buy security for themselves and their enterprises.

Over time, the business of political protection has become increasingly institutionalized. The problem of the Chinese elite, given its vulnerability as an alien group, has been to arrange a durable and reliable system of protection which allows businessmen to calculate costs and to avoid competition among themselves for protection. Uncertainty remains a problem, but the cohesiveness of the Chinese elite and the growth of informal "rules of the game" among Thai power-holders have facilitated two forms of mutual collaboration (Skinner, 1958, pp. 191–192). First, most of the large Chinese commercial and financial enterprises acquired the continuing support of top Thai officials by including them on their boards of directors and thereby entitling them to a share of the profits. Successful promoters of a coup are, of course, most likely to hold such positions. The effect of this device was, on the one hand, to assure Chinese businessmen of political backing for their enterprises. (At worst, it lowered the cost and uncertainties of protection; at best, it afforded preferential access to government contracts and concessions.) On the other hand, the Thai military and bureaucratic elites were afforded added income, opportunities for speculation, and a potential source of patronage. The second form of collaboration involved the hiring of Chinese businessmen with Thai citizenship as managers of public enterprises. In this case Thai leaders were assured of managerial skills while Chinese entrepreneurs acquired a stake in an officially subsidized undertaking.

The process by which business protection was institutionalized is illustrated by the merger of the Northeast Rice Millers' Association and the Thahan Samakki (a soft-drink business under General Phin and the War Veterans' Organization). Following World War II rice millers in northeast

[12] Skinner, 1958, p. 190. This book together with its earlier companion volume, *Chinese Society in Thailand,* represents a comprehensive analytical and historical survey of the Chinese in Thailand.

Thailand were faced with a shortage of transport to Bangkok that set off a fierce competition among the mills in bribing railway officials. As the price of transport reached prohibitive levels, a number of millers organized the Northeast Rice Millers' Association which then secured protection from the Thai political elite by merging with General Phin's Thahan Samakki. The new organization "soon got full control of freight cars on the northeast railway line: squeeze was regularized and allocated among the millers" (Skinner, 1958, pp. 194–195). Analogous forms of cooperation between Chinese business and Thai political power were in evidence in a host of other industries during the 1950s.

The pattern of collaboration between wealth and power described here highlights two essential features of corruption in Thailand. First, it is obvious that such a high degree of institutionalization could only occur in a political system in which both elites are relatively stable. The Thai elite deals with a relatively small and cohesive Chinese elite who can negotiate for much of the Chinese community, while the Chinese, for their part, are dealing with a small number of Thai power figures who, by their authority, can provide fairly regular and reliable protection. Were this not the case, corruption would resemble a Hobbesian struggle for protection and wealth, in contrast to the rather secure form it has assumed. At the top, corruption in Thailand has become a remarkably well organized and systematic operation.

The second noteworthy feature about this pattern of institutional collaboration is that it serves to reduce outright corruption. When a Thai cabinet member joins a Chinese business board, an act that does not violate any law, he substitutes a board member's salary and perquisites for what previously would have taken the form of illegal bribes. In this way the process of influence is moved from corrupt to legal channels. Furthermore, the number of transactions is diminished by the fact that managers of Chinese firms in a given industry now "buy" their protection collectively rather than individually. Many of the same results are achieved by the new pattern as by the old, but the higher degree of institutionalization more often uses legal channels, is more reliable, and cuts down on competitive, piecemeal protection.

In order to thrive, any large commercial venture depends, in Thailand as in early Stuart England, on the personal patronage of members of the power elite. Such protection can provide relief from harassment, extortion, or even arrest, assure routine permits necessary for operation and lead to many government-enforced privileges and concessions that virtually guarantee high profits. Such ties, in spite of their formalization in boards of directors, remain distinctly personal. Every effort is made to personalize the links between a Thai official and a Chinese business leader; the two parties exchange personal visits, make gifts to one another on ceremonial occasions, and so forth. Both individuals in such relationships are themselves important clique leaders with an array of powerful clients in their own community whose interests they protect. The structure of collaboration essentially is reduced to a limited number of personal ties between an individual Chinese leader who acts for his business following and an individual Thai official who acts for his many allies and subordinates.[13] Clique leaders at the apex of each community have in this fashion established durable alliances. Each faction of the Thai ruling elite is affiliated to one set of Chinese commercial interests while each Chinese group is, in turn, linked to a particular clique of Thai leaders. Occasionally, a struggle breaks out, as it did between the Chung-Phao and Yang-Phin cliques over who would control the trade in remittances to China, but efforts are made to restrict the scope of competition. This pattern of alliances has fully integrated Chinese business interests into the patron-client structure of Thai politics.

Overall, contemporary Thailand and early seventeenth-century England manifest striking similarities in the collaboration between power and wealth and the corruption it entails. These resemblances can be traced to economic and political similarities. In both cases the imperfect market system offers few impersonal guarantees to businessmen while tangled networks of monopoly concessions, licensing, and permits leave open few opportunities for profit that are not dependent in some fashion on the government. Politically, the small elites in both systems are organized around personal cliques whose action is seldom restrained either by popular institutions (parties, legislatures) or by class or ideological ties. State officials, for reasons of tradition and political structure, also tended to view a post and its powers as personal possessions that might be used to further the interests of one's family and one's personal clientele. Each context therefore combined a commercial elite that needed protection to survive and a political elite that was both disposed to sell protection and unrestrained from doing so. A strongly politically oriented capitalism emerged in both systems which brought power and wealth elites together at the cost of widespread corruption.

The central difference in the politically oriented capitalism of early Stuart England and contemporary Thailand lies in the relative weakness of wealth elites in Thailand. Their weakness is, above all, a consequence of their status as an alien ethnic group which, notwithstanding the fact that some of its members hold Thai citizenship, is the periodic target of Thai nationalist pressures for expropriation. Even if office were sold in Thailand, their alien status would exclude them from the political mobility enjoyed by commercial elites in England. Operating from an inferior bargaining position, the Chinese in Thailand are easy targets for extortion. If we distinguish bribery from extortion, the Thai situation would therefore exhibit rather more extortion than bribery, while, in seventeenth-century England, the more favorably placed commercial elite bribed just as often as it was extorted.

[13] Skinner (1958, p. 307) identifies seven such "pivotal pairs," of which the three most important at the time were "those between Leader Chung and Police General Phao . . . , Leader Yang and Field Marshal Phin . . . , and Leader Chou and General Sarit."

VARIETIES OF CORRUPTION IN NONPARTY SYSTEMS

5

The patterns of corruption found in Thailand and early seventeenth-century England are recognizable in many less developed nations as well. Such similarities are due, *in part,* to the strength of traditional norms and the comparatively low level of economic development that characterizes preindustrial states. Underdevelopment and tradition underlie at least four of the main structural and value factors that, in the cases examined, were instrumental in encouraging certain forms of corruption. First, traditional norms contribute to a *proprietary view of office* which, in turn, promotes wide discretion in the use of power and the pursuit of personal gain. Second, the persistence of traditional bonds and the formalism of impersonal, legal guarantees make *personal security highly tenuous* unless backed by personal connections and influence. Third, the economic structure of most preindustrial nations means that the *bureaucracy remains a most important avenue for wealth, status, and power.* Finally, the absence of firm institutional guarantees for private wealth and commercial activity perpetuates a situation where *power begets wealth* more easily than wealth begets power.

These four factors are *predisposing* conditions only. The degree to which a political system receives the full blast of these factors depends largely on whether or not extrabureaucratic forces exist which can check them. Generally, such extrabureaucratic forces take the form of political parties. Cohesive ideological parties, such as the Communist Party of the Soviet Union particularly in the early period before it became Stalin's personal instrument, have met with some success in imposing their standards of performance on a vast bureaucracy. Electoral parties, although they may not reduce the level of corruption, do alter its location, beneficiaries, and consequences.

We are dealing here, however, with political systems where the influence of ruling parties or elections is negligible. In this respect Thailand and seventeenth-century England resemble many less developed nations where personal dictatorships, military regimes, traditional monarchies, or nonelective civilian oligarchies hold sway. Corruption in these nations is likely to be reminiscent of the patterns we have examined not only because of the predisposing factors but also because of the nature of political leadership.. That is, such nations are commonly governed by a small elite divided only by personal and parochial alliance networks. Except where such elites or dictators are guided by an ideological vision and have the power to enforce compliance, there are few if any durable outside forces able to suppress the race for spoils or to compel the administration to serve interests beyond its own. Bureaucracies are not simply neutral machines that execute orders. Unless they are directed by outside institutions or ideologies, they tend to become self-serving and parasitical laws unto themselves or simply collections of the leader's personal retainers.

The patterns of bureaucratic self-serving that emerge can be classified under three headings. First, *personalism and patron-client administration* create patterns of favoritism, nepotism, and private gain that reflect the fact that obligations of personal loyalty supersede commitments to law or to institutions. Second, because *administration is politics,* all questions of entry and promotion and virtually all routine decisions are settled by the balance of clique forces and factional interests rather than by regulations or appeals to the public interest. Finally, the absence of any institutionalized bond between the bureaucracy and the public encourages the untrammeled *exploitation of office for profit*,[1] which often involves the regular extortion of the public the bureaucracy presumably serves.

Although we are concerned with corruption, it should be abundantly clear that the pattern we have described permits an entire syndrome of bureaucratic self-serving, of which corruption is but a single manifestation. Other elements in the syndrome, which are continually cited in studies of administration in less developed nations, include: an emphasis on status and rank over productivity or achievement; the ritualization of procedures, in which paperwork and routine become ends rather than means; the absence of any commitment to policy objectives; and the related failure to monitor the implementation of decisions. Similar tendencies exist in any bureaucracy. They blossom most luxuriantly, however, when there is no cohesive party or external control agency to reward attention to productivity and performance and to punish inattention. Administrative corruption is therefore part of a larger pattern of administrative self-serving typical in an autonomous bureaucracy that extracts what it can from the society and is only as obedient, productive, and service-oriented as it must be to preserve its privileges.

Who are the main beneficiaries of this pattern of corruption? Although detailed evidence is lacking, the principal beneficiaries are likely to be: (1) civilian bureaucrats and/or military officers,[2] (2) individuals and groups with parochial (kinship, friendship, ethnicity) ties to military or civilian officials, and (3) wealth elites. That military and civilian officials benefit is patently obvious; they control the administrative and coercive force that represents the basis of the regime. We may expect that those who are related to this elite by kinship or ethnicity will also share the benefits. In more traditional settings, where "market" corruption is *not* common, they may become the most significant outside beneficiaries of corruption. Wealth elites, finally, are principal recipients of favors in most patterns of corruption. Whether they are powerful enough, as in seventeenth-century England, to gain important new advantages and status, or whether, as in Thailand, they seek mostly to preserve a satisfactory status quo, their resources make them valuable allies of the ruling elite.

[1] It goes without saying that many party-dominated bureaucracies are not immune from the private exploitation of offices and from clique struggles. The difference, of course, is that bureaucratic cliques are, in this case, generally the agents and minions of outside political forces.

[2] For military officials one might, in some cases, substitute the monarch and his closest courtiers or the dictator and his closest henchmen.

THE LIMITS OF SELF-SERVING BEHAVIOR

ENGLAND AND THAILAND: THE ENLIGHTENED SELF-INTEREST MODEL

Some bureaucracies are more venal than others. In early seventeenth-century England, before the notion of the public interest became influential, the Crown made efforts to reduce venality in its administration. These efforts were sporadic and largely ineffectual, inasmuch as the Crown's control over its agents was highly tenuous. Nevertheless, partly out of a sense of *noblesse oblige* and partly from a more prosaic concern with the standing of the monarchy in the realm, the Crown often intervened to curb the worst excesses of corruption lest they provide its enemies in Parliament with a convenient issue.

In Thailand as well there is a certain amount of restraint on venality in administration. A total of 4,602 public officials "were discharged, dismissed, or expelled from the civil service between 1954 and 1959, almost 1 per cent per year, for dishonesty and other offenses"(Siffin, 1966, p. 225). While many of these officials were probably "small fish," the elite does deal severely with thefts of public money and with strong-arm extortion methods. The prosecution of some officials together with rigorous controls on overall expenditure exercised by the Ministry of Finance and Budget Bureau do testify to a certain concern for minimum standards of public conduct and for the long-run fiscal health of the nation.

What accounts for even this modest level of self-restraint? First of all, the preoccupation of the Thai elite with fending off foreign intervention has historically been linked with the need to elicit a modicum of public confidence and to avoid indebtedness. There has always been a sense of limits beyond which the elite could not stray without providing one of the great powers with convenient excuse for intervention. That this sense of restraint has endured, however, seems largely due to the relative stability, homogeneity, and institutionalization of the Thai ruling elite. Only an elite which enjoys a measure of cohesion and security can develop a sense of its collective, long-run interest. The appreciation of limits and public obligation that often characterizes a traditional ruling class can thus be viewed as a collective perception of enlightened self-interest which is made possible by the stability of that ruling class over time. In Thailand, corruption and other forms of official self-serving occur within broad limits of a tacit elite consensus about what behavior may be tolerated and what behavior might, if it continued, threaten the position of the entire elite. Not only are these limits reflected in occasional prosecutions for corruption and in fiscal conservatism, but they are also evident in the standardization of procedures for staging coups and in the emphasis on nationalist values in the training of military and civilian officials. Thus, although clique competition within the Thai elite results in a great deal of corruption, it is kept within the broad limits set by the fact that the stability of military/bureaucratic rule in Thailand has fostered the growth of a desire not to kill the goose that lays the golden eggs. Corruption has become increasingly institutionalized and calculable—a genteel pattern of pursuing gain that pays some heed to the continued viability of the regime itself.

INDONESIA, 1958–1965, AND HAITI UNDER DUVALIER: HAND-OVER-FIST MODEL

The mild restraints on the corruption typical of seventeenth-century England and contemporary Thailand are likely to be encountered where elite fragmentation is mitigated by a cultural or class-based homogeneity or by a degree of security that allows power-holders to avoid concentrating on short-run profits. What may we expect, by contrast, in political systems which, like Thailand, are not party-dominated, *but* which, unlike Thailand, are characterized by elites who are highly insecure and highly heterogeneous? The examples of Indonesia under "Guided Democracy" and the tyrannical regime of François ("Papa Doc") Duvalier in Haiti provide extreme but illustrative cases of corruption where limits are virtually absent.

Indonesia From 1958 until the military takeover in October 1965, power in Indonesia was held by a kaleidoscope of military and civilian cliques centering around President Sukarno. The national election of 1955 and the provincial elections in 1957 in Java were the last occasions on which party voting strength was significant and the parliament—though not suspended until 1960—was of only marginal importance by mid-1958. Party leaders were still active, but their relation with their constituents mattered much less now than their personal ties with Sukarno or with the main civilian and military cliques. Most parties, with the exception of the communist PKI, either disintegrated (as parties) or were officially banned. Probably by late 1958, and certainly by 1960, Indonesia was no longer a political system in which political parties held any decisive influence.

Although Indonesia fell into the category of a nonelectoral, nonparty system, it was still not a personal dictatorship under President Sukarno. The flamboyant architect of Indonesian independence did have a wide personal following but he was never able to organize it into a cohesive, let alone monolithic, force. In order to lure as many of his supporters as possible into the National Front, Sukarno was forced to offer concessions that limited his own flexibility. Policy was commonly set by a complex bargaining process between Sukarno, several important cliques, and some powerful individuals.

The ruling group under Guided Democracy was thus a coalition of civilian-military cliques which had their hands full merely maintaining themselves in power and could hardly even contemplate reaching agreement on broad policies (Feith, 1961, p. 380). The army was no exception to this rule. Although it managed successfully to grow in size and to increase its share of the budget, it was internally wracked with dissension compounded by the variety of administrative, managerial, and production functions it had assumed under martial law. Each branch of the military, each regional command, began to develop distinct interests based on its responsibility for a particular portion of the economy. Some residual military unity persisted—mostly on the issue of anticommunism—but political fragmentation increasingly sapped the role of the military as arbiter of the political system. By 1960 Indonesia, like Thailand, was characterized by clique politics except that in Indonesia both the cliques and the alliances among them were much more unstable.

In spite of its deceivingly authoritarian forms, Guided Democracy was thus a *weak* form of coalition politics. The inability of the coalition to curb the increasingly disastrous inflationary spiral from 1961 to 1965 is striking evidence of this weakness. Stabilization policies would have entailed austerity budgets for many clique-controlled sectors of the government and jeopardized the coalition itself; no one was strong enough to impose a solution and the inevitable consequence was a growing budget deficit that met the short-run needs of all, while eating away the very foundations of the regime (Mackie, 1967, pp. 19–21).

Corruption was common in Indonesia under parliamentary cabinet rule, but under Guided Democracy it attained truly epidemic proportions. The desire for patronage jobs and funds, which had always been a significant factor in the decisions of most political parties, became the absolutely controlling factor under Guided Democracy, since parties were now completely divorced from the collective demands of their mass constituents.

Much of the corruption of the early 1960s centered around three related arenas: the intra-government clique struggles for wealth and patronage; the growth of bureaucratic capitalism; and bureaucratic extortion of members of the public. In the first arena the military-bureaucratic cliques encouraged budget deficits to increase the spoils at their disposal. Each clique overspent in order to increase its members' income and to swell with its own supporters the administrative rolls of agencies it controlled, regardless of how incompetent those supporters may have been. Informal commissions were exacted from foreign suppliers, civilian and military leaders let contracts to firms in which they had an interest, government equipment and supplies were sold on the black market, uncooperative subordinates were summarily dismissed, and so forth. The evidence of lavish standards of consumption, expensive foreign cars, and rumors of bank accounts abroad suggests that such corruption paid handsome dividends.

Guided Economy, the economic program of Guided Democracy, marked the ascendancy of nationalized or government-connected enterprises as an important arena of corruption. The process of nationalization was as often motivated by the desire of important cliques for new fields of patronage and revenue as by a set of nationalist or socialist policy goals. Even as the economy as a whole declined, politically oriented businessmen with the right connections were able to accumulate large fortunes on the strength of the protection and special import licenses afforded them. A powerful group of "palace millionaires" thus emerged. Their methods included bribing for state-guaranteed economic privileges and for protection of their black-market sales, lavish gifts to ministers, conspiring with bureaucrats in the falsification of accounts and inventories, and a variety of other corrupt practices designed to assure profit with safety.

The absence of any external controls on the administration encouraged a parasitic orientation toward the public. Those with cash or clique connections might fare quite well, but without such resources one was doomed to the caprice or extortion of officials bent on private gain. Amid the growing welter of economic regulations, both low- and high-ranking officials extracted what profit they could from their position. Their own salaries greatly eroded by inflation, officials extorted payments for expediting a claimant's case, for issuing necessary permits and licenses, for arranging an appointment with a superior—in short, for any service that was of value to citizens. The branches of administration that, like the police, dealt more in sanctions than in services, used the threat of punitive action to extort money and goods from the public. In general, the cumulative tariff exacted by bureaucrats for services prompted the Indonesian observation that "under Guided Economy the price of an article is determined not by supply and demand but by the number of officials through whose hands it must pass" (Feith, 1967, p. 391).

While the forms of corruption in Indonesia in the early 1960s differed little from practices in Thailand, what is distinctive about the Indonesian case is the total volume of corruption and the absence of any limits. In particular, we can differentiate corruption in Indonesia from corruption in Thailand along at least four dimensions. First, impressionistic but persuasive evidence clearly indicates that corruption was more extensive in Indonesia. At the lower levels of administration, the corruption which was merely common in Thailand was virtually universal in Indonesia, where payments were exacted for almost every service and where government property was regularly sold on the black market. At the top, more Indonesian officials seemed to amass personal fortunes in a comparatively shorter time than is the case in Thailand. Second, the scramble for funds and patronage within the Indonesian bureaucracy was, unlike the situation in Thailand, not confined inside the boundaries of fiscal soundness. On the contrary, steeply inflationary budgets were the rule rather than the exception throughout the period of Guided Democracy.[3] Third, coercive forms of extortion from the public represented a much larger share of total Indonesian corruption than of Thai corruption. Whereas strong-arm extortion was often detected and punished in Thailand, the Indonesian police and civil service regularly extorted cash and goods from the public with little risk of prosecution. Fourth, in contrast with the highly institutionalized forms of corruption that appear in Thailand, corruption in Indonesia was much more unsettled—not to say chaotic. The organization of joint business boards of local officials and Chinese capitalists has not occurred in Indonesia to the extent it has in Thailand. One expert estimated that "corruption in Indonesia has not become as thoroughly 'institutionalized' as in Thailand, where the appropriate bribes for different services were well-known, regular, and predictable" (Mackie, 1967, p. 86). The chaotic pattern of corruption in Indonesia also meant that it was more unreliable. Bribers got what they paid for in Thailand, but in Indonesia the corruption "market" was so disorganized that "prices" were highly unstable and "delivery" by sellers was highly uncertain.

The chaotic hand-over-fist pattern of corruption in Indonesia results, in part, from the lack of security and cohesion of its elite in this period. Thai clique struggles, after all, take place in a relatively secure and settled context that allows the elite to display a minimum level of decorum which enhances the regime's long-run interests. By contrast, the utter fragmentation of the Indonesian elite prevented it from imposing even modest limits on the tempo or forms of self-seeking.

The insecurity of the Indonesian elite was even more debilitating than its fragmentation. This insecurity was evident both in the constant "retooling" of civil servants and ministers who suddenly fell from favor, and in the shakiness of the entire regime. Even if one somehow managed to keep one's personal footing, there was no assurance that the structure itself would last; both personal careers within the regime and the survival of the regime itself were in constant jeopardy.[4] Long-term goals were out of the question. At

[3] To some degree the deficits were also linked to military needs during the PRRI rebellion in the outer islands and the West Irian campaign. Deficit levels at 1960 constant prices are given in Mackie, 1967, p. 8.

[4] One should add here that insecurity of office in Indonesia was exacerbated by the high stakes of politics. Whereas in Thailand those who lost their high posts in a coup generally remained in the ranks of officialdom, the Indonesian elite had no such assurance. The institutionalization of intra-elite politics in Thailand approximated a restricted conflict in which losers could be participants in the next "round." The very rules of the game in Indonesia were in jeopardy and it was understood that losers might be eliminated altogether.

the political level this instability expressed itself in a succession of short-run patchwork solutions designed to ensure immediate survival; at the personal level it expressed itself in the corrupt exploitation of office to maximize short-run personal gain.

The general principle involved here is simply that, other things being equal, *the more uncertain and insecure the environment, the shorter the period over which individuals seek to maximize gains.* Under conditions of great uncertainty, those who pursue long-run strategies are penalized while those who pursue short-run strategies, where risks are smaller and more calculable, are more likely to succeed.

In this context, the relationship between security of tenure and exploitation of an official post has long been recognized. Seventeenth-century monarchs preferred the sale of an office to its rental because a buyer acquired a stake in the long-run profitability of his office whereas a renter would normally squeeze as much as possible out of the post while he held it, ignoring the long-run effects of his behavior. The implicit analogy here with a business enterprise is not amiss. One would not expect prudent businessmen, for example, to invest in long-range activities that tie up fixed capital where instability and uncertainty abound. The rational course, instead, is for the businessman to minimize his risks by concentrating on short-run, high liquidity, commercial transactions. And this is precisely what the majority of entrepreneurs in underdeveloped nations do. Political and bureaucratic entrepreneurs behave in much the same manner. In Indonesia, the great insecurity of both career and regime—brought about by the severe fragmentation within the elite, an uncontrolled and deteriorating economy, and external factors as well—thus contributed to a short-run, exploitationist view of office and to rampant corruption.

Haiti The example of Haiti under the tyrannical personal dictatorship of Duvalier is introduced here as a limiting case—one where the pattern of corruption reflected both the insecurity of the regime and the terrorism it employed to survive.

Sharing the Caribbean island of Hispaniola with the Dominican Republic, Haiti is the most densely populated country in the western hemisphere and suffers from the lowest per capita income as well. Its heavily eroded agricultural lands produce but a bare subsistence for the illiterate peasantry, while the entire economy supports a national budget of only $35–40 million for a population of over 4 million. Economic prospects are further dimmed by the mass exodus of intellectuals, professionals, and technicians.

Since its independence in 1804 Haiti's political history has been a series of dictatorships, each of which ended in the assassination or exile of one dictator and the installation of another. Duvalier, who came to power in 1957, was the third black dictator since the overthrow of the mulatto elite in 1946. Although he made skillful use of African folk religion (vodun or voodoo) to buttress his regime, Duvalier's dictatorship was based largely on the use of terror and coercion. To escape complete dependence on the army—the ruin of his predecessors—he created the *Tonton Macoute*, an irregular armed force of toughs that functioned as his personal instrument of terror and assassination.[5] While no firm figures are available, political murders and beatings were common in Haiti and those suspected of conspiring with exiled plotters were summarily executed. The army was neutralized by frequent reassignments, demotions, expulsions, and occasional blood purges.

The use of the term "personal" for Haiti's dictatorship is meant to convey the uninstitutionalized character of Duvalier's rule. The entire civil service—if one can call it that—was appointed, promoted, and dismissed by the president in the same way he managed the *Tonton Macoute*. A National Assembly, consisting of fifty-eight handpicked favorites who were fraudulently installed, existed but exercised no authority. From top to bottom Haitian officials served only at Duvalier's personal pleasure. Politics, in this context, became a factional struggle among Duvalier's chief lieutenants—including his family—for the continuing favor of the President. An official's physical survival, let alone his tenure in office, depended on convincing Duvalier of his utter personal loyalty and devotion.

Government is virtually the only source of wealth in Haiti. Given the uninstitutionalized, coercive basis of the regime and the absence of any limits—either legal or traditional—predatory corruption was virtually unchecked. The annual budget, composed mostly of customs and excise taxes, was the dictator's personal purse to dispose of as he saw fit. Loyal retainers and family members were given personal gifts, the *Tonton Macoute* was rewarded for its missions of intimidation and death, personal fortunes were created, and so forth. Additional irregular revenue was extorted by Duvalier's personal police for the *Mouvement Renovation Nationale*, which was nothing more than a personal fund for the President's use. On their own, the *Tonton Macoute* as well as civilian and military officials were free, so long as they enjoyed Duvalier's confidence, to extort what they could from the public.

Although corruption under Duvalier bore some resemblance to that of the other regimes we have examined, the Haitian regime in its entirety was an almost unique case. Like the Indonesian elites, the tenure of Haitian officials was highly insecure, as was the regime under which they held office. Like seventeenth-century England, the personal authority of the ruler weighed heavily in the political system and a good deal of the corruption was centralized and organized at the top. But here the similarity ends, for the traditional limits and institutional restraints under which the British Crown labored were totally absent in Haiti. Duvalier was restrained neither by traditional norms nor by the power of an independent aristocracy—nor by any other institutionally based center of power. Finally, the Haitian regime

[5] See Graham Greene's fictionalized account of Haiti in *The Comedians* (1966).

rested to a much larger degree on violence and coercion than does any other system we have described. It would not be an exaggeration to compare the Haitian regime to that of a strongman with his band of armed followers who have managed to seize the government and have proceeded to use their monopoly of force to squeeze as much as possible from the treasury and the populace.

Corruption in Haiti was therefore distinguished by its reliance on physical threats and coercion, by the absence of any institutional or traditional restraints on what was permissible, and by the radical insecurity of the regime and its officials which encouraged the exploitation of office for personal gain. If any regime may be said to have been *fundamentally* corrupt, it would be the Duvalier regime.

REGIME AND CORRUPTION

The pattern of corruption in each of the regimes we have examined is different. Some of these differences are due to unique historical circumstances that make generalizations difficult. At another level, however, the pattern of corruption is affected by the degree of instability and fragmentation of the elite in a way that permits some tentative generalizations.

Given the difficulty of collecting quantitative evidence on corruption, Table 5–1 should be treated as a schematic presentation of hypotheses. The relationships suggested there appear to fit the cases we have already described, but the evidence is still too sketchy to allow a rigorous testing. Table 5–1 reflects an estimate that both fragmentation and instability will increase the over-all level of corruption. The instability of the Haitian regime (reflected in blood baths and purges) and the fragmentation of the Thai elite thus make for fairly high levels of corruption regardless of the former's dictatorial leadership and the latter's stability. When instability and fragmentation are both present, as in the Indonesian case, levels of corruption are likely to be especially high.

With respect to the type of corruption, the table reflects the proposition that either strongman rule or stability will produce some "order" in corruption. Under strongman rule, corruption at the top is unlikely to occur but, when it does, it is likely to be patterned, while under fragmented but stable rule, the elite is likely to collectively enforce some limits governing what is permissible.

The location of corruption, irrespective of its over-all level, shows very little variation. As the uniform statements about lower echelon corruption indicate, it is difficult for any nonparty regime to deal effectively with corruption in its lower bureaucracy. Stable military regimes such as Nasser's Egypt may initially have succeeded in inspiring and enforcing high standards even at the lower rungs of administration, but the absence of any deeper or

Table 5–1 Patterns of Corruption in Nonparty Regimes *

	Cohesive Top Elite (Strongman)	*Fragmented Elite (Clique Structures)*
Relatively stable (reformist or traditional regimes with some institutional backing)	e.g., Early Ayub Khan Pakistan, Early Nasser Egypt, Early Ataturk Turkey Level of corruption: Moderate-low Type: Relatively organized (if it occurs) at the top; atomized and unpredictable below Location: Less at top, somewhat more below	e.g., Postwar Thailand, Early Stuart England (Ethiopia, Iran, and Morocco in 1970) Level of corruption: Relatively high Type: Relatively atomized and unpredictable, *but* with some limits and ground rules, especially at top Location: Common at top and below
Relatively unstable (based on coercion or short-term coalition building)	e.g., Duvalier Haiti Level of corruption: Very high Type: Relatively organized at top; atomized and unpredictable below—extortion common Location: Common at top and below	e.g., Guided Democracy, Indonesia 1958–1965 Level of corruption: Very high Type: Very atomized and unpredictable with few limits or ground rules —extortion common Location: Common at top and below

** Although the table takes a dichotomous form, it is obvious that the main variables of instability and fragmentation are questions of degree. A particular regime may thus belong midway along a continuum of fragmentation or instability rather than at one pole. The Thai elite, for example, may be less fragmented than the Moroccan elite, and one would need to make the necessary allowances for this in predicting patterns of corruption.*

institutionalized value changes will tend to erode away the initial gains. The only developing nations which appear to have durably reduced corruption in the lower bureaucracy have been a few single-party states that have created a trained and devoted cadre to staff such positions (e.g., North Vietnam, Singapore, Tunisia).

The relatively stable regimes in Table 5–1, whether fragmented or not, tend to develop some restraints on the over-all level of corruption and on the form it takes. In the case of fragmented but rather stable elites, this restraint results from a shared devotion to enlightened self-interest and a *noblesse oblige* sentiment among a small elite class. For relatively stable strongman regimes in underdeveloped countries, this restraint in practice has depended upon the support of a reformist military. Evidence suggests, however, that the restraints generated by military rule are likely to ebb as the military is increasingly fragmented by the fruits of power.

We can also now assess the effects of these different patterns of corruption on administrative control and economic development. The Indonesian pattern under Guided Democracy, both analytically and empirically, would seem the most injurious to both. When, as in Indonesia, the elite is severely fragmented and unrestrained by traditional or institutional norms, it becomes literally incapable of implementing broad policies. Neither administrative units nor individuals can be monitored or controlled; unrestrained black markets for government services abound, local and subordinate units sabotage policy at will, and *de facto* decentralization turns each unit into an autonomous satrapy. Efforts at fiscal stabilization, state marketing, and personnel reduction in Indonesia were foredoomed by the fragmentation of the elite. The insecurity of the regime and of individuals within it prevented the growth of predictable, centralized corruption. In this atmosphere, long-run private sector investment all but disappeared as it was impossible to secure reliable protection at a calculable price. The debilitating effects of such anarchic corruption is evident in the precipitous inflation and declining productivity (outside the agricultural sector) in the last four years of Guided Democracy. Where corruption is more institutionalized, as the Thai case shows, economic growth is possible; under Indonesian conditions it was impossible.[6]

PARACHIAL AND MARKET CORRUPTION

As ideal types, "parochial" (nonmarket) corruption is a situation where only ties of kinship, affection, caste, and so forth determine access to the favors of power-holders, whereas "market" corruption signifies an impersonal process in which influence is accorded those who can "pay" the most, regardless of who they are.[7] The real world, of course, rarely ever contains such pure cases. The proportion of market to parochial cor-

[6] Even the Haitian case does not seem *a priori* to preclude growth as surely as does the Indonesian. In practice, though, the overpopulation and the exhausted land of Haiti make any economic advances unlikely. The difference is thus that Indonesia starts with some natural potential while Haiti has virtually none.

[7] The term "pay" here is not exclusively confined to cash transactions. Payments in kind (both goods and services) are just as common and can be considered as falling into the "market" category as they can generally be assigned an equivalent cash value. As we have also indicated, political resources are made more or less valuable by the nature of the political system. Thus in an electoral setting like the Philippines, control over a bloc of votes is a viable resource for seeking favors, while in Thailand control over votes is not as important as command over a key military unit.

ruption, and hence the pattern of beneficiaries, varies widely among underdeveloped nations. In Thailand, for example, corruption seems to involve a high component of straightforward bidding procedures—or "side payments" of a fixed amount for all who seek an identical favor. The Diem period in South Vietnam, by contrast, was characterized by the marked preference in access accorded Catholic ex-northerners, although market corruption was by no means absent.

Inasmuch as parochial corruption reflects narrow, traditional loyalty patterns while market corruption offers access to all who can pay, one might expect that long-run trends would favor the more "modern" market form. There is some evidence, as we have shown, for this trend in seventeenth-century England. Such predictive statements, however, go beyond our present knowledge and ignore the possibility that corruption may remain the arena of parochial ties precisely because such ties are not accorded a legitimate place in the formal, modern political system.

We can nonetheless identify certain conditions under which the extent of market corruption (absolutely and as a proportion of total corruption) is likely to increase. First, and most obviously, the growth of a large commercial elite with little formal access to influence will raise the volume of money bribes offered for favorable government decisions. Second, the greater the scale of government activity, other things being equal, the more widespread market corruption will become. This is so because large-scale government entails many transactions where no personal ties exist between the bureaucracy and members of the public. In this context, the use of cash and other material incentives becomes more likely. The prime locations of much market corruption in developing nations corroborate this point. It is precisely in those areas of government activity involving a large number of small transactions—the issuance of driver's licenses and permits for village market stalls, the settlement of minor criminal charges, the acquisition of seats or freight space on railroad cars, to mention but a few—that "price" corruption is most common. Over time, it is also in these areas that market corruption tends to become institutionalized so that there is a widely known and rather stable price for a particular action. By contrast, the market in large transactions involving such benefits as import permits or large construction contracts is likely to show less price stability and a greater intrusion of parochial considerations.

The different patterns of access to influence created by each type of corruption may have quite divergent political consequences. A specialist in India has concluded, for example, that popular discontent is much more likely to develop against parochial corruption that excludes some castes or communities than against market corruption that grants access to all who can pay (Weiner, 1962, p. 236). If indeed market corruption—as exemplified by the minutely calculated amounts every subcontractor for Indian Railways must pay to a half-dozen officials (see *Report of the Railway Corruption*

Enquiry Committee, 1955, p. 48)—is less disturbing to the public than caste or ethnic favoritism, this is surely a reflection of the predominant cleavages in Indian society. *The test, then, is whether the predominant form of corruption cuts across or reinforces existing cleavages.* Ethnic-based corruption would accordingly be more politically disruptive in an ethnic-oriented society than in a class-oriented society; and conversely, class-oriented market corruption would be more disruptive where class conflict was paramount and less disruptive where ethnic conflict was decisive. Finally, for the developing nations, one must not ignore the frequent coincidence of wealth and ethnicity. Where this is the case, market corruption will consistently favor one ethnic group simply because a single ethnic group controls most of the society's wealth. In practice, then, access by virtue of wealth may have precisely the same impact as parochial corruption.

CORRUPTION AND ECONOMIC DEVELOPMENT

Many of the distinctions we have made in analyzing corruption are of consequence for assessing its impact on economic growth. In Thailand and seventeenth-century England corruption and proto-corruption may actually have assisted economic growth, whereas in Indonesia and Haiti they clearly stifled it. The propositions that can be extracted from our analysis, however incomplete, to account for this disparity are presented below:

Corruption is obviously less likely to seriously retard economic growth when:

1. National rulers are either uninterested or hostile to economic growth.
2. The government lacks the skills, capacity, or resources to effectively promote economic growth.

and when:

3. Corruption is "market" corruption where all "buyers" of influence have equal access to bureaucrats and politicians. (The assumption here is that if parochial considerations are weak, only the ability to pay will count and efficient producers will have more of an advantage.) [8]
4. Corruption benefits groups with a high marginal propensity to save (e.g., wealth elites) more than groups with a low marginal propensity to save (voters)
   —this situation is, in turn, more likely in a noncompetitive political system than in a competitive one where votes can be traded for influence.
5. The cost of a unit of influence is not so high as to discourage many otherwise profitable undertakings.

[8] This assumption is invalid for many countries where a few huge firms whose volume of business is so great that, regardless of their efficiency, they can outbid more efficient small producers.

—this situation is more likely when there is price competition among politicians and bureaucrats who sell influence.

6. There is greater certainty as to the price of a unit of influence and a high probability of receiving the paid-for "decision."
   —this is more likely when:
   a. The political and bureaucratic elites are strong *and* cohesive
   b. Corruption has become "regularized"—even institutionalized after a fashion—by long practice.
7. Corruption serves to increase competition in the private sector rather than to secure a special advantage or monopolistic position for any one competitor.

It should be clear that most of these contingencies are not met in less developed nations. Even though the public sector in these nations is notoriously inefficient, the parochial and unpredictable pattern of corruption and the emphasis on securing state-guaranteed monopolies that characterize corruption in most of these nations are hardly conducive to economic growth.

ELECTORAL CORRUPTION
THE BEGINNINGS OF MACHINE POLITICS
6

NEW BENEFICIARIES

Finally in the last two decades of the Republic the trading in votes rose to such a height that the law was repeatedly strengthened. . . . By an act of 67 B.C. *the "treating" of voters was made punishable. . . . In 55* B.C. *a new law struck at what was probably the most flagrant form of corruption. . . . The wealthy candidate would quietly arrange for his election to the desired office with a band of political "go-betweens"* (interpretes). *These professional gentlemen would proceed to mark out the Roman tribes into smaller and more wieldy sections, arrange voters into clubs and fraternities, compound with each section for its votes, marshal the faithful henchmen to the electoral* comitia, *and duly pay over the stipulated honorarium upon delivery of the election.*[1]

The growing rewards of office in an affluent Rome, together with a Roman citizenship policy that expanded the electorate, created the conditions for an embryonic form of machine politics. Although political parties (*facio, partes*) consisted merely of allied patrons and their followings, the *interpretes* were the lineal ancestors of the "borough-monger" of late eighteenth-century England and the "precinct captains" of urban American machines. The Roman Republic thus provides an early example of broad electoral corruption which contrasts to the pattern of corruption typical of monarchical or military-bureaucratic regimes.

The most striking consequence of electoral competition for public office is that it widens the arena of public influence. Ordinary voters come to control a valuable political resource; the giving or withholding of their votes makes a difference in the fortunes of those who seek to manage the state. Competitors for office will vie with one another to gain votes and voters will use their franchise to secure some gain. Inducements to voters may or may not take corrupt forms. If voters are moved by traditional loyalties, their rewards are symbolic; if they are moved by broad policy choices, they may be attracted by legislative promises. But if, as with many "new" electorates, the desire for immediate tangible gain predominates, candidates will find it difficult to provide effective inducements without violating formal standards of public conduct. The pressures to win a majority following make it likely that, in the short run at least, a party will respond to the incentives that motivate its clientele rather than attempt to change the nature of those incentives.

It is not astonishing, then, to find that an early rise in electoral corruption may actually indicate the growing independence of popular choice. The decline of terrorism, outright fraud, and landowners' control over the peasantry in Philippine elections, for example, was accompanied by a quite noticeable increase in vote-buying by candidates.[2] No longer able to threaten

[1] Davis, 1910, p. 13. See also Taylor, 1961, especially pp. 1–75.

[2] Wurfel, 1963, pp. 770–771. Wurfel gives an excellent account of the role of money in Philippine elections.

voters physically or to stuff ballot boxes on a scale sufficient to win, candidates and parties were obliged to proffer material rewards as a means of persuasion. The decisiveness of material incentives in the absence of force or fraud at a certain stage of political development can also be seen in Lincoln Steffens' vivid portraits of urban political machines in the United States at the turn of the century. The Philadelphia machines distributed their material rewards less widely than other city machines because their leaders could fix electoral results through force and fraud. New York's Tammany machine, by contrast, was a system of "democratic corruption" in which a much greater portion of the population shared because the public's voting power was not diluted by fraud or coercion (Steffens, 1963, pp. 139, 203, 205).

Would-be influencers seek out the real decision-makers of a regime; as the identity and location of these decision-makers change, so does the flow of corrupt transactions. Inasmuch as a party system changes the focus of political decisions from the administrative to the party elite, it shifts the pattern of corruption to the advantage of party leaders. The more dominant the party elite, the more it potentially benefits. Important commercial interests in India, for example, which had provided illegal salary supplements for a good many key civil servants prior to independence, now divert a portion of those funds to Congress Party politicians who currently make many of the crucial decisions. A similar shift occurred during the last stages of colonialism in other underdeveloped nations.

Electoral systems not only affect the locus of influence. They affect its legal status as well by providing noncorrupt channels for influence that simply do not exist in autocratic systems. For a businessman to give money to a civil servant is generally illegal, whereas the same amount given to a politician's campaign fund may "buy" just as much influence over government decisions but is quite proper. The party system thus provides not only a legitimate way for those affected by decisions to give power-holders money, but also legitimate ways (e.g., legal patronage, pork-barrel legislation, private member bills, etc.) for power-holders to influence voters by means of tangible rewards. The over-all level of corruption (legally defined) is not necessarily lower in party systems, but the party system generally does legitimize certain patterns of influence that could only occur corruptly in a military/bureaucratic system.

We can now summarize a number of the proposed relationships between the political system and the pattern of beneficiaries of corruption. Table 6–1, though suggesting only rough comparisons, offers a convenient summary of a portion of the analysis.

Military/Bureaucratic Polities As we have dealt at some length with such regimes in Chapters 4 and 5, little additional explanation is required. The nonelectoral, nonparty character of the Thai regime, for example, means that those who control coercive force (military)

Table 6–1 Pattern of Beneficiaries from Corruption by Group and by Type of Political System in Less Developed Nations

	Recipients of Benefits *				
Type of Political System	Individuals and Groups with Parochial Ties to Power-Holders	Wealth Elites	Bureaucrats/ Military	Party Leaders and Cadre	Voters and Vote Brokers
Bureaucratic/military Polity (e.g., Thailand until 1971; post-1965 Indonesia)	x	X	X		
Party-dominated Polity—noncompetitive (e.g., Guinea until 1966; Ghana 1960–1965)	x	x	x	X	
Party-dominated Polity—competitive (e.g., Philippines until 1971; India until 1971)	x	X	x	X	X

* *Large X's indicate the probable major beneficiaries of corruption in each type of political system, while small x's indicate minor beneficiaries. The over-all level of corruption is not a factor in this table, but only the distribution of benefits from whatever level exists. Thus it is conceivable that a minor beneficiary in one system might, because the over-all level was quite high, actually receive more benefits than a major beneficiary in another system with less corruption.*

or administrative power (bureaucracy) and their personal clienteles are the central beneficiaries of corruption.

Noncompetitive Party Regimes Most one-party noncompetitive regimes, apart from the special case of communist states which is not examined here, have developed in Africa, and the pattern in Table 6–1 largely reflects this fact.[3]

The central role of the party that characterizes such regimes is likely to mean that party leaders and cadre will share fulsomely in whatever corruption exists. Not only has the party generally politicized many decisions that might otherwise be administrative issues, but it often needs a large stock of rewards to weld the party together and overcome the centrifugal forces of ethnicity, family, region, and so forth. To the extent that ideological cohesion

[3] Given the spate of military coups in less developed nations over the past decade, this category may prove ephemeral. By far the best assessment of such regimes is in Zolberg 1966.

within the party is lacking, a network of rewards may provide organizational cement.[4] Many such rewards can be furnished legitimately; many cannot.

Table 6–1 indicates that wealth elites will probably benefit less in this kind of regime than in the other two types. This assessment is based on the fact that such regimes have usually shown a marked preference for the expansion of the public sector at the expense of the private sector. Where this is so, both the size and influence of extragovernmental wealth elites is diminished.[5]

Competitive Party Regimes Whereas the power-holder in an autocratic regime has no special reason to disburse rewards beyond what suffices to maintain his alliances with a few powerful men, the power-holder in a competitive electoral context has great incentives to disburse rewards to those voters whose ballots will determine who takes power. Such rewards may, and often do, take the form of local development programs,[6] pork-barrel legislation, loan programs, and legal patronage, but the resort to more irregular inducements is also common. This is especially so in less developed nations where narrow family and kin-group rewards are very persuasive.

The more hotly contested the elections, the greater the distributive effort is likely to be. Elections are generally all-or-nothing affairs and uncertainty over the outcome will raise costs; when the race is close, the marginal utility of the additional dollar of campaign funds (or patronage promises) is all the greater. In this fashion, competing parties must often, in return for campaign contributions which they deploy to attract votes from the general public, make commitments to assist the policy interests of their big commercial patrons once they achieve office. The series of transactions involved in this three-cornered relationship frequently assumes corrupt forms.[7]

The outstanding example of corruption in a competitive electoral context is, of course, the Philippines. Direct per capita campaign expenditures

[4] Here one might contrast Tanzania (TANU) and Tunisia (Socialist-Destour) party systems where ideological cement is important—and hence corruption less widespread—with Ghana 1960–1965 (CPP) or the Ivory Coast (PDCI) where the personal character of the party regime appears to be less effective in curbing corruption.

[5] In such venerable one-party states as Formosa (Kuomintang) and Liberia (True Whig Party) this is clearly not the case.

[6] Many development programs, particularly local community development efforts, serve important electoral functions for governing parties in new nations. Anomalies that confound the observer when such programs are analyzed as rational economic plans to raise productivity disappear once they are seen as, above all, efforts to build effective electoral machines on particularistic bases.

[7] The party in power has a tremendous advantage in that it can use state funds to reward some of the electorate and can often do this quite legally. "Out" parties, on the other hand, must rely either on less certain promises of rewards when and if they win, or on immediate bribes to voters and vote-brokers.

are the highest in the world as a proportion (1.6 percent in 1961) of average per capita income and are equal to 13 percent of the national budget. A realistic accounting would also have to include the immense pork-barrel funds (400,000 pesos per senator, 200,000 per congressman) used for electoral purposes and the cash given to the 10–20 percent of the electorate that actually sells its vote. National candidates distribute much of their campaign fund to local and regional supporters, who in turn distribute funds to *barrio* (village) leaders, friends, relatives, and other potential allies. One can appreciate the significance of this "trickle down effect" by the fact that a common laborer will often receive the equivalent of an entire month's wages for his vote (Wurfel, 1963, pp. 761–769). Knowing that meeting the electorate's short-run, material claims is the price for a continuation of policies that allow their commercial interests to thrive, wealth elites provide (openly and covertly) a large share of the campaign funds. The conjunction of highly competitive elections, powerful wealth elites outside government, and an electorate that is no longer automatically loyal to its local patrons but has not yet developed strong, horizontal, class or occupational ties has conspired to make the Philippines something of a model of electoral corruption.

EARLY ELECTORAL PATTERNS

LATE EIGHTEENTH- AND EARLY NINETEENTH-CENTURY ENGLAND

As the Philippine example indicates, patterns of electoral corruption are closely related to the structure of the electorate itself. The managers of any competitive electoral party have an intuitive grasp of the "structure of the voting public," in the sense that they know what appeals and what incentives are most appropriate to each group of voters.

Candidates and party strategists in England from the mid-eighteenth to the mid-nineteenth centuries were also faced with the task of organizing, or, to use the term then employed, "working," the electorate of each constituency. By relating the electoral strategies of this period to the structure of the English electorate, we can appreciate the highly individual pattern of inducements that typify most elections in pre- and early industrial settings. For in spite of the limited size of the English electorate—even after the Reform Bill of 1832 only one adult male in seven acquired voting rights—the kind of voting public to which English parties appealed was not so different from electorates in many new Asian and African nations.

In classifying English voters, a central distinction is the extent to which they were free agents and, if they were, whether they were motivated by short-run inducements or by larger policy issues. Those who were, by and large, *not* free agents we have termed "locked-in electorates"; those who were more nearly free agents but oriented to short-run gains we have termed "potential machine electorates"; and those who were oriented to broad policy issues we have termed "issue electorates."

Locked-in Electorates Close to one-fourth of the English members of parliament were returned from rural county (as opposed to borough) constituencies where much of the electorate was controlled by one or more of the dominant landowning families. In most areas, despite the large agricultural wage-earning class produced by the commercialization of agriculture, rural society was intensely localized. Within each parish, strong links of mutual obligation still bound tenants and craftsmen to the large landholders. This dominance was an amalgam of traditional patterns of allegiance reinforced by the ascendant economic position of the leading families. Small holders may have been in theory independent, but they often rented a portion of their land and, in any case, wished to maintain good relations with the local elite (Walcott, 1956, pp. 9–10).[8] If tenants did not themselves see their interests as identical with those of their landlords, economic pressures could be deployed to bring them into line.

The "locked-in electorates," whose votes were virtually predetermined by existing economic arrangements, were by no means confined to rural county areas although that was where they bulked most heavily in election outcomes. In many of the smaller parliamentary boroughs, the adjacent landowner's economic power was often decisive in the choice of candidates. Especially by the mid-nineteenth century, however, new centers of economic power controlled substantial portions of the electorate in borough constituencies. As one historian puts it, "Employers influenced their contractors, manufacturers their workpeople, masters their servants, breweries their tied houses . . ." (Gash, 1953, p. 175). In the absence of effective working-class organization, and particularly in slack times when labor was abundant, such instructions carried considerable weight.

There was no sense in parties or candidates appealing directly to "locked-in electorates." By definition, these were voters who could be mustered most easily by coming to terms with their landlord, their employer, or their master who could deliver their votes in the election. Electoral corruption and bribery generally arose in these constituencies under two conditions. First, competing leading families occasionally disagreed about candidates and launched an electoral struggle for supremacy which involved bribing

[8] Although Walcott is describing the situation a few decades earlier, it is largely applicable to most of the period we are describing. Landlord pressures were no doubt greatly facilitated by the fact that balloting before 1872 was not secret but open, thereby making it easier to detect nonconformity and take reprisals.

the constituency's floating vote. Knowing the ruinous costs of such contests of strength, however, potential competitors made every effort to reach a prior settlement. Second, the ruling family(ies) of a county could, and occasionally did, decide to "sell" the seat it (they) controlled for cash, patronage grants, or other considerations. In this event, prospective candidates or party managers could strike a bargain directly with the local patron(s).

The central feature of "locked-in electorates" is that they were seldom the object of large-scale bribery. Especially in rural areas where such electorates were often decisive, the voter was connected to the larger political system through his agent-patron whose control over his political will was a function of his control over his means of subsistence. Whatever corruption existed centered around the bargaining of patrons among themselves or with the outside world. There is no need to bribe someone who is not a free agent.

Early Machine Electorates The county constituencies where much of the electorate was locked in to traditional patrons may be contrasted with many of the borough constituencies where the electorate's choice of candidate was not so completely predetermined. Here the opportunity for "purchasing" a seat in Parliament depended less on winning the favor of a few landlords than on the financial and patronage resources at the disposal of the prospective candidate. On the one hand, there were the small electorates of the "burgage boroughs," in which the vote was attached to certain pieces of real property, and the "corporation boroughs," in which an often closed corporation of one hundred men or less formed the electorate. Bribery and corruption in these boroughs centered around the competition to buy the votes of corporation members or to buy the houses or plots of ground that carried the valuable franchise. The electors of New Shoreham's corporation borough, for example, collectively organized " 'The Christian Society,' which sold the seat to the highest bidder and then distributed the proceeds among the electorate" (Wraith and Simpkins, 1963, p. 66). On the other hand, there were quite a few larger boroughs—often termed "freeman boroughs"—where, even before 1832, the franchise was quite extensive. Here the votes of artisans, small shopkeepers, and even laborers could not be ignored by any candidate.

It was in these larger boroughs that large-scale electoral corruption was most frequently found. The venality of these electorates was in large part a function of their relative freedom from the economic and social pressures that operated on most "locked-in" rural electorates. As a noted historian has observed,

> . . . *corruption in populous boroughs was the effect of a citizen status in an electorate not fully awake to national interests; even so it was a mark of English freedom and independence,* for no one bribes where he can bully *[Namier, 1961, p. 4; emphasis added].*

This explains why electoral corruption was, if anything, more common immediately after the 1832 Reform Bill than before; as the control of the landed oligarchy declined and new urban voters were extended the franchise, there was a gradual "democratization" of corruption in which candidates dealt increasingly with citizens whose votes were not predetermined from above. As late as 1868, in the election following the second Reform Bill, there is a striking direct correlation between the size of a borough's electorate and the election expenses of the winning candidate. Bribes to voters formed a large share of these expenditures. Among portions of the middle class, artisans, and even laborers there were "issue-oriented" voters for whom class or collective local interests loomed large but, particularly in the large boroughs, they were swamped by voters with shorter-range interests.

For many voters in large boroughs, the franchise was considered an important financial asset. "Payments" for votes took a variety of forms. Among the most common were free drinks, meals, and entertainment, merchandise certificates redeemable through local merchants, the hiring of large numbers of nonworking committeemen, contributions to church and charitable groups, direct cash bribes, and finally the traditional distribution of "head money" after the election by the winning candidate. Frequently "treating the voters" assumed an aura of mere patronly hospitality which put a social cosmetic on bribery so as to preserve everyone's self-respect. Even candidates who could anticipate an easy victory were expected to meet their obligations to the voters, but it was in close races where the demand for votes inflated their value that campaign expenses reached staggering levels. The price per vote generally increased as election day neared, and many voters, sensing the market, waited almost until the polls closed to cast their votes in close races. There were constituencies in which over two-thirds of the voters were bribed. In boroughs where bribery was widespread, a new career developed for political entrepreneurs: that of the "borough-monger." The borough-monger set about organizing a large group of electors and, acting as their buyer, negotiated a price for that bloc of votes with a candidate-buyer.[9]

In addition to the purchasing of votes as election day approached, successful candidates learned that they might enhance their chances considerably by "nursing" a constituency between elections. The prospective candidate might contribute to local charities, offer to fix the town clock, found a school, or pay for some needed public works improvements. More particularistic forms of patronage were also significant. An MP often had a say in the awarding of local patronage jobs and could thereby create a personal organization that would work on his behalf between elections. Candidates,

[9] The system is quite similar to the "butty system" of employment prevalent at the time, in which laborers were organized into gangs with a leader who negotiated on their behalf with prospective employers to set wage rates and conditions of work. During this period, such small-scale brokerage may have been the most efficient means of recruiting both laborers and electors.

in short, made every effort to create a solid base of support well before the campaign began. Both the electors and the city fathers, for their part, looked on the MP as an important source of loans and gifts between elections. The electoral patronage network thus brought into being by private wealth and the manipulation of office was not perhaps as durable as the more coercive control of a landlord over his tenants, but it often proved as effective in winning elections.

The venality of the large borough electorates did not stem merely from their poverty, for rural tenants were just as poor. It stemmed rather from the combination of their poverty and their relative independence. Because they were not "locked-in" as were rural tenants, they could trade this relative margin of political (voting) power for urgently needed goods, services, or cash. One can, in fact, view these constituencies as arenas in which the poor traded political power for cash while rich candidates traded wealth for power. The effect of this tacit bargain was, of course, a certain redistribution of income at election time (Gash, 1953, p. 113).

A second effect of elections in corrupt boroughs was the infusion into Parliament of new wealth elites. Had it not been for the corrupt borough electorates, the domination of Parliament by the landed classes would have been more difficult to break. From the 1830s through the election of 1880—which was "probably . . . the most costly election ever held in Britain" [10]—candidates expenses increased greatly, and, as the costs rose, so also did the political prospects of the very wealthy *vis-à-vis* the older elites. A Tory clergyman expressed the fears of many of the latter when he testified before the Election Committee of 1853 that "bribery was steadily increasing, 'swamping the intelligence and property of the country' " and allowing Parliament to be taken over by "an oligarchy of capital." [11] Just as the sale of office had aided political mobility in the seventeenth century, so the virtual sale of Parliamentary seats provided political mobility in the nineteenth.

Electoral Coordination of Government Machinery

The existence of a potential machine electorate is a necessary but not sufficient condition for the creation of a political machine. A political machine, as the term implies, requires a sufficient centralization of control over the key inducements of campaign funds, spoils, patronage, etc., to produce a relatively disciplined electoral organization that is capable of regularly winning elections. The obstacles blocking the creation of a political machine in

[10] Gwyn, 1962, p. 51. Gwyn (p. 51, n. 3) cites estimates of total costs between £2.5 and £3 million, which comes to approximately £1 per elector. The election occurred, moreover, in the midst of an "agricultural depression and general price decline."

[11] Gwyn, 1962, p. 77. This is, of course, why much of the older elite backed anti-corruption measures.

Britain from 1750 to 1850 were formidable. First, the persistence of a good many patron-dominated constituencies throughout this period afforded their representatives a measure of independence from party discipline. Second, and far more important, the limited resources parties or ministries could deploy forced them to rely upon independently wealthy candidates who could finance their own campaigns and were hence less amenable to party discipline.

The resources available to a particular government for engineering elections were, on balance, rather meager. Beyond a small amount of cash that might help win a few close races and a number of safe seats in seaports and garrison towns, the government had only marginal control over recruitment into Parliament. Thus it had to come to terms both with independent patrons whose local base of power was secure and with an increasing number of MPs from *la grande bourgeoisie,* whose ability to buy seats made them resistant to government discipline. The funds a government could give its candidates were seldom more than a small fraction of their electoral expenses. When we add to this the highly fractionalized nature of political parties which compounded the problem of central coordination, the difficulties of election management by the ruling party, let alone the opposition, can be fully appreciated.

Unable to determine who entered Parliament, the ruling party made efforts to use its patronage and rewards to create a majority within Parliament. The Duke of Newcastle, by adapting and improving on Walpole's methods, succeeded in patching together a Whig parliamentary machine in the 1760s. Since few of the MPs with whom he dealt had been elected on their policy stands, he could lure many of them into voting for the government by the award of contracts, pensions, and patronage posts. Namier's research indicates that the most loyal Whig MPs tended to be those who were financially linked to the government; of the 558 members elected in 1761, fully 260 were, in Namier's term, "placemen" (Namier, 1961, p. 72). The central role of patronage in cementing parliamentary majorities did not disappear quickly. It continued to be a staple means of coordination throughout much of the nineteenth century and became marginal only after the Acts of 1883–1884.

It was possible, then, to create something of an embryonic machine *within* Parliament. Such coalitions were highly fragile affairs, for the party leadership was never in a position to deny nomination or election to many of its adherents. Lacking this crucial means of machine discipline, they were forced to bargain with a host of relatively independent members who might bolt the coalition—at relatively small cost to themselves—whenever they became dissatisfied with their share of spoils or saw more promising opportunities in joining the opposition. The party leadership simply did not command the preponderance of power and material resources that would serve to fashion a disciplined and durable political machine.

FRANCE UNDER LOUIS NAPOLEON

The importance of a centralized administration and a concentration of political resources (patronage, funds, etc.) for the creation of a large machine can be seen in the political edifice constructed in France by Napoleon III between 1852 and 1869.[12] Due in part to the centralization that occurred under the First Empire, the central government not only had a large and disciplined administrative apparatus but also controlled a vast store of grants, patronage posts, and contracts which it alone awarded. Skillfully coordinating these political resources, Louis Napoleon managed to build a powerful electoral machine.

The material inducements that held this electoral coalition together were both collective and individual. A commune that elected an administration candidate received government grants for its budget while opposition communes were "starved out." The large pool of individual rewards at the disposal of the government-appointed mayor and subprefects—including the notarization of legal forms, the approval of petty licenses, and the letting of minor contracts and public works jobs, to mention a few—were systematically deployed to enhance the government's electoral position. Prefects within this system became powerful, well-disciplined regional bosses who deprived the traditional ruling class of its former patronage resources. Louis Napoleon had both the centralized resources and the administrative sinews to create a machine.

Louis Napoleon's success depended on both a rural electorate that was "machine-workable" and a sufficient pool of patronage resources to "work it" so as to elect his own men to the National Assembly. His machine far outdistanced that of Newcastle in at least two respects: first, it broke the hold of landowning patrons over their locked-in clients by denying them some of the local powers they had retaken since the Revolution, while creating a more formidable alternative patronage network through its own officialdom; and second, its resources in many electoral districts allowed it to assure victory to its candidates *without* its having to select independently wealthy nominees who could finance their own campaigns. The government's nominees were often "new men" (lawyers and former officials) who were dependent on the state's patronage and financial resources for their election. Compared to Newcastle's allies, therefore, Louis Napoleon's men formed a more centralized and disciplined political unit which, given its reliance on material incentives, resembled the political machines of a later era.

The political system of the Second Empire also reflects the limits of machine coordination. Napoleon III's electoral organization was based largely on rural votes, whereas the urban areas remained bastions of re-

[12] The source for this description is Zeldin, 1958.

publican opposition to the regime. The growth of class and ideological loyalties (i.e., of issue-electorates) in the large cities, especially of course Paris, made their electorates relatively impervious to machine-style blandishments. Like the Irish Home Rule supporters in the late nineteenth-century (cf. O'Brien, 1957) or the staunch trade unionists of the early Labour Party, the French urban voters were often too conscious of their collective interests to respond to individually distributed short-term benefits. If the French urban electorate was more issue-oriented than its English counterpart in this period, French rural voters—also because of the Revolution—were more detached from the power of local clergy and nobility than English rural voters and were therefore more susceptible to electoral manipulation. The potential machine electorate in Newcastle's England was to be found among the recently enfranchised urban voters, while in Louis Napoleon's France it was in the countryside.

It is evident from these examples that the characteristic machine inducements—patronage, pork-barrel, bribes—are only effective in certain contexts. Their impact is minimized, on the one hand, when a great many voters are still closely tied to traditional patron-landowners who control their means of subsistence and hence their votes. Their impact is minimized, on the other hand, when the growth of ideological or class loyalties and concerns (including religious and nationalist interests) fosters an orientation to broad policy goals as distinct from short-run material gains. If correct, this analysis implies that it is especially among new electorates for whom traditional vertical ties have weakened, but have not yet been replaced by new ideological or class ties, that machine politics is most likely to flourish.

MACHINE POLITICS AND THE SOCIAL CONTEXT OF POLITICAL TIES

Our descriptions of machine electorates has suggested that the patterns of political beliefs and loyalties that prevail among voters in large part determine whether or not a political machine can emerge. That is, a voting population with certain characteristics is a necessary, but not sufficient, condition for the growth of machine parties. In this section we will attempt to make the analytical implications of the preceding descriptions more explicit.

The progression described in Table 6–2 focuses on changes in the nature of loyalty ties with which any political party that desires to win elections must grapple. It is tailored to a bargaining context—particularly, electoral bargaining—and is less applicable where force or threats of force are the main basis of cooperation. Nothing is intended to be rigidly deterministic about the movement from Phase A to B to C. The phases are, however, based largely on the empirical experience of the United States, England, and the new nations.

Table 6–2 Changes in Loyalty Ties and Party Inducements *

Phase A	Political ties are determined largely by traditional patterns of deference (vertical ties) to established authorities. Material, particularistic inducements to cooperation play a minor role except among a limited number of local power-holders.†
Phase B	Deference patterns have weakened considerably in a period of rapid socioeconomic change. Vertical ties can only be maintained through a relationship of greater reciprocity.‡ Competition among leaders for support, coupled with the predominance of narrow, parochial loyalties, will encourage the widespread use of concrete, short-run, material inducements to secure cooperation. The greater the competitive electoral pressures, the wider the distribution of inducements is likely to be. Influence at the enforcement stage is common.
Phase C	New loyalties have emerged in the process of economic growth that increasingly stress horizontal (functional), class, or occupational ties. The nature of inducements for political support are accordingly likely to stress policy concerns or ideology. Influence at the legislative stage becomes more appropriate to the nature of the new political loyalties.

** The broad lines of this schema were suggested to me by an analysis of the use of money in elections contained in Heidenheimer, 1963, especially pp. 808–809.*

† Traditional ties generally allow some scope for bargaining and reciprocity; the possibility that clients might flee to another jurisdiction, and labor and defense needs that make the implied contract in the classical feudal tie between lord and serf recognizes this modicum maintenance of a sizable clientele desirable, provide subordinates with some leverage. The of reciprocity. The distinctions made here in the degree of reciprocity are therefore relative. See for example, Foster, 1963.

‡ What appears to happen in the transitional situation is that the client is less "locked-in" to a single patron and the need for political support forces patrons to compete with one another to build larger clienteles. For a brilliant analysis of this pattern in Philippine politics, see Lande, 1965, passim.

Although the phases in Table 6–2 have been separated for the purpose of conceptual clarity, they are likely to overlap considerably in the empirical experience of any nation. It is thus a question of which loyalty pattern is most common and which less common. Within new nations all three patterns typically co-exist; rural villagers may remain deferential to their traditional leaders, recent urban migrants may behave more as free agents seeking jobs or cash for their votes, while a small group of professionals, trade union leaders, and intellectuals may perhaps be preoccupied with ideological or class concerns. Even fully industrialized nations may contain recalcitrant, usually isolated pockets where deference patterns have not yet yielded to other modes of political expression.[13]

[13] In this context party labels are deceptive. Parties proclaiming ideological or class positions are often found in rural areas where the labels have been appropriated *in toto* in a continuation of essentially traditional feuds between powerful families and their respective clienteles. The key is the nature of loyalty patterns, not the name of the organization. See Levi, 1965.

Prior to fuller treatment later, a brief word is in order concerning the process of change implied by the model. Movement from Phase A to Phase B involves the shaking loose of traditional deference patterns, which can occur in a variety of ways. For the United States large-scale immigration by basically peasant populations was often the occasion for this change; for England and the continent the extension of the suffrage, urban migration, and the commercialization of the agrarian economy marked this transition; while for less developed nations the economic changes introduced by colonial regimes, universal suffrage, and rapid migration from village to city has provided the catalyst. The social disorganization that resulted was often exacerbated by ethnic, linguistic, or even caste cleavages, but similar patterns have arisen in the Philippines, for example, amid comparatively homogeneous populations.

Elections themselves have of course played a central role in this transformation in that they placed a new political resource of some significance at the disposal of even the most humble citizens. The transition from Phase A to Phase B is also marked by the rise of a new class of patrons—the new bourgeois commercial and industrial elites, party and government officials. These new patrons, reflecting the economic changes underway and the growing role of the state in society, tend to replace traditional tribal or landowning patrons of an earlier time.

Movement from Phase B to Phase C would appear to depend on the process of industrialization as new economic arrangements take hold and provide new foci of identification and loyalty. As the case of the United States illustrates, though, the presence of sharp ethnic and sectional cleavages—the latter reinforced by a federalist constitutional structure—may for a long time considerably dilute the strength of these new bonds.

The duration (and geographic scope) of Phase B, when the social context is most hospitable to machine-style politics, may vary widely. When the social disorganization accompanying urbanization and economic change is particularly severe and of long duration, when it is compounded by deep cultural differences,[14] and when competitive elections with universal suffrage are introduced early, the pressures toward machine-style politics will be vastly greater than when demographic change is gradual and less severe, when it occurs with a minimum of cultural cleavage, and when the electorate is restricted. The historical circumstances of both the United States and many new nations have been, in this sense, more conducive to the development of machine politics, than, for example, the experience of much of western Europe.

[14] Only in circumstances where ethnic groups do not feel threatened with physical or cultural extinction do ethnic cleavages promote machine politics. Where the threat is perceived as great, the result is often collective solidarity, as in the case of the Irish Home Rule militants or the Ibos of Nigeria.

CONTOURS OF THE MACHINE MODEL

Periods in which traditional ties are eroding, the voting public growing, and urban migration accelerating are likely to stimulate a host of small-scale material (often family-centered) demands. Such demands, as we saw in Chapter 2, can seldom be given legislative form. A party that wishes to mobilize such an electorate will find that neither appeals to traditional loyalties nor appeals based on modern ideological or broad policy concerns are likely to command much attention. Coming to terms with such an electorate requires a different kind of party.

There is a party form that not only has been able to respond to particularistic interests but has thrived on them. I am, of course, referring to the urban political *"machine,"* a form that flourished in the United States around the turn of the century. Although now virtually extinct, the machine party once managed, in immigrant-choked cities, to fashion a cacophony of concrete, parochial demands into a system of rule that was at once reasonably effective and legitimate. As urban America was *par excellence* the cradle of party machines, an understanding of the contours and dynamics of machine parties is best gained by examining this form in greater detail. It will be recognized at the outset that the machine form can occur only in certain political settings. At a minimum, the setting of the machine requires:

1. The selection of political authorities through elections.
2. Mass (usually universal) adult suffrage.
3. A relatively high degree of electoral competition over time—usually between parties but occasionally within a dominant party.

These conditions reflect the fact that since machine politics represents a distinctive way of mobilizing voters, it arises only in systems where getting out the vote is essential to gaining control of the government. While these conditions are necessary for machine parties, they are by no means sufficient, as we shall see below.

Beyond these preconditions, the essential features of most machines are reasonably clear.[15] Normally applied to a political party in power, the term "machine" connotes the reliable and repetitive control it exercises within its jurisdiction. What is distinctive about the machine, however, is not so much its control as the nature of the organizational cement that makes such control feasible. The machine is not the disciplined, ideological party held together by class ties and common programs that arose in continental Europe. Neither is it typically a charismatic party, the cohesion of which depends on a popular belief in the almost superhuman qualities of its

[15] Some of the more successful efforts at careful description and analysis include: Key, 1936; Mandelbaum, 1965; Miller, 1969; Banfield and Wilson, 1965.

leader. The machine party is rather a nonideological organization interested less in political principle than in securing and retaining political office for its leaders and distributing income to those who run it and work for it (Banfield and Wilson, 1965, p. 116). It relies on what it accomplishes in a concrete way for its supporters, not on the broad policy stands it might take.

"Patronage," "spoils," "bribery," and "corruption" are inevitably associated with the urban machine as it evolved in the United States. As these terms indicate, the machine party deals almost exclusively in *particularistic* (i.e., individual and small-scale) *material rewards* to maintain and extend its control over its electorate. Although pork-barrel legislation provided inducements for ethnic groups and neighborhoods collectively, the machine did most of its favors for individuals and families. The very nature of these rewards and favors naturally meant that the machine party became *specialized in organizing and allocating influence at the enforcement stage.* The corruption it fostered was not the product of random greed but was finely organized to maximize its electoral support.

The machine party is thus best characterized not only by the degree of its electoral control but also by the distinctive resources that knitted it together. Ties based on charisma, coercion, or ideology were often minor chords of machine orchestration; the "boss" might be viewed as a hero by some, he might use hired toughs or the police now and again to discourage opposition, and a populist ideology might accompany his appeals. For the machine party, however, such bonds were definitely subsidiary to the concrete particularistic rewards that represented its staple means of political coordination and distinguished it as a form.

The vaguely populist image of the machine party was based less on its pronouncements of general policy (which were rare) than on a myriad of acts that symbolized its accessibility, helpfulness, and desire to work for "the little man." It meant a great deal to an immigrant or laborer cast adrift in a *laissez-faire* state to know that when and if he needed help, the local ward boss would do what he could. For the rank and file, the machine boss represented a patron of those at the base of the social pyramid; whereas the court system, with its rational system of justice, may have favored property interests, the boss typified for them an "empirical justice" "that works more consistently in the interests of the poor, for attention is focused upon their concrete needs and deprivations" (Edelman, 1964, p. 118). Hints—even exposés—of municipal corruption and graft were winked at or actually applauded by the machine clientele as the social banditry of an urban Robin Hood. The long-run consequences of his acts for the city were largely ignored. More than most types of political leaders, the image of the boss and his party was fashioned from concrete acts (a job, a gift, help with the police, relief).

Given its opportunistic concern for remaining in power, the machine party was a responsive, informal context which facilitated bargaining based on reciprocity. Leaders of a machine party were rarely in the position of dictators; those who supported them did so on the basis of value received or anticipated. The machine party for the most part accepted its electoral clients as they were and responded to their needs in a manner that would elicit their support. It could respond to new groups and adapt to highly dynamic situations.

The implication to be drawn is that the machine-style party can be distinguished from other regimes by the basis of its authority. A machine, in this sense, is a *special case of a regime that bases its authority largely on its distributive activity* (service, "effectiveness"). It is to be distinguished, first, from regimes—whether based on traditional authority, on charismatic authority, or on coercion—that require less distributive capacity. The distinctiveness of the machine party, however, lies not simply in its reliance on distribution, but also in the nature of its distributive activity. The machine typically distributes benefits in the form of patronage, pork-barrel, and corruption to individuals, small groups, neighborhoods, and certain business enterprises. This pattern clearly demarcates it from distributive regimes (including many with an ideological basis) that devise general legislation and welfare measures to meet the concrete demands of whole sectors of the population, such as occupational groups, classes, age categories, and so forth. *A machine regime may thus be characterized as one in which traditional, charismatic, and coercive authority are less significant than distributive activity, and in which distributive activity is particularistic rather than collective.*

LOYALTY AND INDUCEMENTS

Political parties generally must offer inducements of one kind or another to potential supporters. The sort of incentives most likely to "move" people is contingent, as our phase model implies, on the kinds of loyalty ties that are most salient to the potential client. Elaborating on this relationship between loyalty bonds and party inducements, Table 6–3 suggests the most likely empirical patterns.

Parties in the real world commonly confront all four patterns of loyalty simultaneously and fashion a mix of inducements that corresponds to the mix of loyalties.[16] Inducements, moreover, are often multi-purpose: public works

[16] The importance of one or another pattern can, in addition, be amplified or diminished by structural characteristics of the formal political system; in the United States, for example, federalism and local selection of candidates tend to amplify geographical ties. See Lowi, 1967.

Table 6–3 The Relationship Between Loyalty Bonds and Party Inducements

Nature of Loyalties	*Inducement*
1. Ties of traditional deference or of charisma	Protection and symbolic, nonmaterial inducements *
2. Community or locality orientation (also ethnic concentration)	Indivisible rewards; public works, schools, "pork-barrel"; communal inducements
3. Individual, family, or small-group orientation	Particularistic material rewards; patronage, favors, cash payments, "corruption"; individual inducements
4. Occupational or class orientation	Broad material rewards; policy commitments, tax law subsidy programs, etc.; "general legislation"; sectoral inducements †

** Charismatic ties naturally involve more purely symbolic inducements than do ties of traditional deference, in which clients are generally assured a certain minimal level of material well-being (security) by their protector or patron in return for their loyalty.*

† Term borrowed from Banfield and Wilson, 1965, p. 337.

that benefit a locality also usually carry with them a host of jobs and contracts that can be distributed particularistically. Similarly, job patronage can be wielded so as actually to favor an entire community or ethnic group.

With these qualifications in mind, I am suggesting that, given pressure to gain support, a party will emphasize those inducements that are appropriate to the loyalty patterns among its clientele. Although material inducements are as characteristic of occupational or class loyalties as they are of local or family loyalties, what is unique to the machine system is simply the scope and nature of the group being "bribed" by the party, not the fact of "bribery." In the case of occupational or class loyalties, the inducements can be offered as general legislation (and rationalized by ideology, too), whereas inducements at the individual or family level must often be supplied illegally (i.e., corruptly) at the enforcement stage.[17] The classical machine faces a social context in which narrow community and family orientations are most decisive. Responding to its environment, the machine party is likely to become consummately skilled both in the political distribution of public works through pork-barrel legislation and in the dispensation of jobs and favors through illegal channels.

[17] Political systems vary in the extent to which favors and patronage can be carried out within the law. In the United States the traditional use of postmasterships, ambassadorial posts, and a number of state jobs exempt from normal civil service requirements provides a pool of party spoils which are *legally* denied parties in India, Malaysia, or Nigeria.

Historically, the expansion of the suffrage together with the rupture of traditional economic and status arrangements have signaled the rise of particularistic, material inducements. This transition is evident in the contrast between the "locked-in" county electorates and the larger, turbulent borough electorates in early nineteenth-century England.

A similar shift from patterns of deference to patterns of short-run material inducements is evident in contemporary Philippine politics. Like the English landed proprietor before the late eighteenth century, the Filipino *haciendero* could, until recently, rely on his tenant laborers and on peasants indebted to him to vote as he directed. Increasingly, though, the economic arrangements and traditional patron-client ties that ungird this deference are eroding, and the peasant now often requires cash or other special inducements in exchange for his vote. Deference patterns are weakest where social change has been greatest. Pork-barrel legislation is still of great electoral significance, but family and individual inducements (to the exclusion of broader, sectoral demands) are the real currency of electoral struggles. Party platforms are not taken seriously because Filipino voters know that individually they can escape the effects of laws that disadvantage them as a class, and that their vote can be traded for cash, a temporary job, or hospital care (Lande, 1965, pp. 43, 115). As elsewhere, the decline in deference in the Philippines has encouraged the growth of machine-style politics in which a mixture of public works and, above all, family-centered material rewards provide the fuel. The necessary incentives, as our description indicates, are generally arranged by influence at the enforcement stage—reflected both in the widespread corruption and the absence of structural reform for which the Philippines is noted. Philippine experience, in this regard, is reminiscent of changes in the conduct of American politics in the mid-nineteenth century. Until then more paternalistic patterns had prevailed, with voters generally deferring to the wishes of established local notables. Only after such traditions of deference had receded in the face of economic change and immigration could the machine style of particularistic, material rewards begin to thrive on a large scale.

At this point we should distinguish between machine-style parties and the creation of a dominant political machine. Given an electoral system and a voting public that is oriented to machine-style rewards, it is likely that machine-style parties will develop, but whether a dominant machine party develops is another matter. The creation of a dominant party machine depends not only on effective organization and leadership but, more important, on the location of control over machine-style inducements. Only when it is possible for party leadership to gain command over the distribution of most patronage, contract, and financial resources can it exercise effective control over subordinates and "starve out" the opposition. Machine bosses were thus constantly concerned with avoiding a fragmentation of their patronage resources. Where this was not possible, where the patronage was not fully in the boss's hands, where a separation of powers or jurisdictions made it possible for the opposition to retain some resources and patronage slots, a kind of feudalized machine-style politics developed that precluded the dominance of a single party.[18] America was a classical example of this feudalistic development, for the control of a city machine was often undercut by federal, state, or even county patronage which was not within its jurisdiction. Local machines, often shaky affairs, were possible, but national machines were not. It is therefore the location of control over machine inducements that is crucial in forecasting whether machine-style politics will produce a dominant party machine. The loyalty patterns we have described may be sufficient to produce machine-style electoral strategies, but they are not sufficient by themselves to produce a dominant machine.

Changes in modal patterns of loyalty help account not only for the growth of machine politics but also for its decline. In addition to other factors (which will be discussed later), the growth of political ties in which family and small-group bonds were less important than before, and in which occupational and/or class ties were more prominent, undercut the very foundation of the machines.[19] The specific inducements which the machine was organized to supply worked their "magic" on a smaller and smaller proportion of the electorate. Instead, as businessmen and laborers each come to appreciate their broader, longer-run interest as a sector of society, they increasingly required general legislation (collective bribes) that met their group interest in return for political support. Here and there a social context tailored to machine politics remained, but either the machine party reconciled itself to the new loyalties—becoming less and less a machine party in the process—or it was the electoral victim of social change. Parties continued to offer palpable inducements to voters, but the new inducements were more typically embodied in general legislation, whereas previously they had been particularistic and often outside the law.

[18] It was for this reason that reformers sought to weaken the powers in the hands of the mayor—a strategy with enormous long-run costs of which we are only now becoming aware.

[19] Most immigrants to the United States, for example, at first "took for granted that the political life of the individual would arise out of family needs . . ." (Hofstadter, 1955, p. 9).

THE MACHINE IN COMPARATIVE PERSPECTIVE

7

The applicability of the "machine" political form to many parties in the new states has been noted by quite a few political analysts. In this chapter we shall compare the contextual factors that gave rise to the machine in the west, particularly in the United States, with conditions in less developed nations and examine the comparative role of patronage distribution in building party unity.

Analyzing the dominant parties of West Africa after independence, Zolberg (1966) has described them as political machines. The development of the Congress Party in India has likewise been compared to American machine parties, and one expert (Weiner, 1967) has gone so far as to recommend the "machine" to Indian politicians as a form to emulate.[1] The particular machine qualities these social scientists find in parties in Africa and Asia include their ability to adjust demands from disparate groups of supporters on the basis of bargaining and self-interest, their capacity to respond to social change through informal (often corrupt) mechanisms, and finally their potential for stability and popularity in a context scarcely hospitable to either.

What these writers have done, in effect, is to construct an analogy between the social context of political parties in Africa and Asia on the one hand, and late nineteenth–early twentieth-century America on the other. In the United States, the rapid influx of new populations for whom family and ethnicity were the central identifications, when coupled with the award of valuable opportunities for profit (streetcar and electric power franchises, supply and construction contracts, etc.) and an expanding public payroll, provided the ideal soil for the growth of party machines. Developing nations could be viewed as offering a social context with many of the same nutrients. New governments had recently acquired control over the disposal of lucrative posts and privileges. They faced electorates that included many poor, newly urbanized peasants and a lumpenproletariat which could be easily swayed by concrete, material incentives. The point these observers make is not only that the social context typical of most new nations tends to promote machine qualities in ruling parties, but also that the machine party is a suitable and relatively democratic political formula that can manage such a complex environment. Given elections and a certain social context, so their reasoning goes, the price of effective political cooperation—at least in the short run—involves meeting the narrow demands, often through patronage, favors, and bribery, that are the hallmarks of machine politics.

THE ECOLOGY OF MACHINE POLITICS

The distinctive style of political coordination embodied in the machine has historically occurred in settings where—in addition to rapid social change and competitive elections—(1) political power was somewhat fragmented, (2) ethnic cleavage and/or social disorganization were widespread, and (3)

[1] See also for India and other developing nations Bailey, 1963; Bretton, 1966; and Feith, 1962.

most of the population was poor. Drawn mostly from studies of urban machines in the United States, these characteristic features of the environment of machine politics seem in large degree applicable to many underdeveloped nations in which political parties have resembled machines.

PARTIAL FRAGMENTATION OF POWER

If, within a city or nation, resources and power are extremely fragmented, the leader of a single unit will find that beyond his immediate area it is difficult to amass the coalition-building resources to create a machine. If, on the other hand, power and authority are extremely centralized, the leader will find it as easy to coerce as to bargain. Machine development is most likely, therefore, in a situation where there is enough concentration of resources to prevent the creation of independent feudal domains but not so much as to allow the central authority to dictate terms to the petty leaders with whom it must deal.

One searching account of the development of machine politics in Chicago lays particular stress on the multiplicity of urban authorities and jurisdictions within the city.[2] The city's eight main "governments" created so many jealously guarded centers of power that a mayor faced a host of potential veto groups, any one of which could paralyze him. He could secure cooperation with these authorities only by striking informal bargains—often involving patronage, contracts, franchises—and thus putting together the necessary power piece by piece.

Power was fragmented in yet another sense. Party candidates did not face one electorate but many; each had its own demands and a successful campaign depended on assembling a temporary coalition based on inducements suited to each group. The mayor's resources were only sufficient to bring a tenuous order to this confusion. His temporary authority rested on his continuing capacity to keep rewards flowing at an acceptable rate.

New York in the era of Boss Tweed strikingly resembles early twentieth-century Chicago. In spite of the prodigious manipulations attributed to him, Tweed was not especially powerful and had little control over party branches, which remained free to nominate their own candidates for many posts. By an adept use of patronage and the city debt he did, however, manage for a time to create a finely articulated political coalition. Assessing the nature of Tweed's feat, one student of the period Mandelbaum, 1965, p. 58) concludes,

[2] Merriam, 1929, pp. 68, 90. Merriam's analysis is particularly valuable as he was simultaneously a political scientist and a politician throughout the period he describes. See also the empirical description in Gosnell, 1968. Gosnell provides the first breakdown of favors and assistance given out by precinct captains and develops an explanation for the rise and fall of machines.

There was only one way New York could be bossed in the 1860's. The lines of communication were too narrow, the patterns of deference too weak to support freely acknowledged and stable leadership. Only a universal system of benefits—a giant payoff—could pull the city together in a common effort. The only treasury big enough to support coordination was the public till.[3]

Many leaders of developing nations might well sympathize with Tweed's difficulties. They also face a highly differentiated populace—not only divided along ethnic, religious, linguistic, or regional lines, but also representing various stages of incorporation into the modern sector and varying degrees of loyalty or hostility to the nation-state. Except in those instances where physical coercion is preferred and is sufficient to the task, rulers in the new states, in order to govern, must reach some accommodation with many of these interests. Electoral pressures naturally increase the value of such accommodations. But even the leaders of a one-party state with a populist ideology are under some pressure to maintain popularity with a sizable portion of their citizenry. More often than not the price of rule involves paying off each of a variety of interests in their own—usually particularistic—coin. The system of coordination thus comes to resemble machine politics.

SOCIAL DISORGANIZATION AND INSECURITY

The immigrants who constituted much of the clientele of the American urban machine came largely from the European peasantry. As such, they were quite unfamiliar with their new urban-industrial setting and could hardly be expected to approach the party system as an independent or confident citizenry. Just as the fragmentation of power made it advantageous for the politician to offer special inducements for support, so the situation of the immigrant made him eager to respond to blandishments that coincided with his most immediate needs. Machine inducements are thus particularly compelling among disoriented new arrivals who value greatly the quick helping hand extended to them by the party.[4]

The dependence of machine parties on a clientele that is both unfamiliar with the contours of the political system and economically on the defen-

[3] See also Flynn, 1947, p. 21, for a twentieth-century account of New York City politics in which a similar argument is made.

[4] Immigrants and new arrivals in the city are not the only ones who are grateful for machine favors. At the other end of the spectrum one might place the large enterprises whose financial success depends on state or city decisions and who therefore support the machine. In this group one might include the historic relationship between railroads, oil interests, large mining concerns, and utilities and many state and local machines. Unlike the immigrant-machine relationship, however, the entrepreneur-machine connection is more nearly one between equals and involves legislative favoritism more often than petty favors.

sive is underscored by the character of the small pockets where vestiges of once powerful machines still exist. One recent example was the Dawson machine (really a "submachine") in Chicago. This machine has rested squarely on favors and patronage among the Negro population, most of which has come to Chicago from the rural south within the last generation. Deprived of even this steadily diminishing social base, the machine has elsewhere withered as the populations it assisted became acculturated and could afford the luxury of wider loyalties and longer-range political goals. The Dawson machine was itself threatened by the growing appeal of collective goals within the black community.

It is no coincidence, then, that machines flourished during the period of most rapid urban growth in the United States. In such periods the sense of community was especially weak and social fragmentation made particularistic incentives virtually the only feasible means of cooperation. The machine bound its clientele to it by virtue of the employment, legal services, economic relief, and such benefits which it could offer. "For the lower strata, in return for their votes, it provided a considerable measure of primitive welfare functions, personalized help for individuals caught up in the toils of the law, and political socialization" (Burnham, 1967, p. 286; Merriam, 1929, p. 173, also calls the precinct worker "something of a social worker not recognized by the profession"). Many of the machine's favors were nonmonetary and involved showing a man where to apply for a job or housing, how to fill our legal forms, and who to go to in case of trouble. It was the immigrant's newness to the country and his insecurity, quite as much as his poverty, that drew him to the machine—and the machine to him.

With few qualifications, the social context that nourished machines in America matches conditions in new nations. Rapid urban migration of rural peasantries, especially since World War II, when coupled with ethnic fragmentation, economic insecurity, and a basic unfamiliarity with the western governmental forms adopted by most new states, has conspired to create an analogous social context. As in the United States at the turn of the century, a large clientele is available that will respond enthusiastically to short-run material incentives and to the party which provides them.

POVERTY

Perhaps the most fundamental quality shared by the mass clientele of machines is poverty. Machines characteristically rely upon the votes of the poor and naturally prosper best when the poor are many and the middle class few. Studies have shown that for American cities "the lower the average income and the fewer the average years of schooling in a ward, the more dependable the ward's allegiance to the machine" (Banfield and Wilson, 1965, p. 118). Poverty shortens a man's time horizon and maximizes the effectiveness of short-run material inducements. Quite rationally he is willing to accept a job, cash, or simply the promise of assistance when he needs it, in return for his vote and that of his family. Attachments to policy goals or to an ideology imply both some degree of future orientation and the presence of wide loyalties, whereas poverty discounts future gains and focuses unavoidably on the here and now.

The attitudes associated with poverty that facilitate machine-style politics are not confined to just a few urban centers in less developed nations, but typify portions of the rural population as well.[5] In such circumstances, the jobs, money, and other favors at the disposal of government represent compelling inducements. Deployed to best advantage, these incentives are formidable weapons in building coalitions and/or in electioneering. The ease with which votes are purchased—individually in many urban areas, and in blocs where village or ethnic cohesion facilitates it—during elections in the new nations is a measure of the power of short-run material rewards in the social context of poverty.

PATRONAGE EMPLOYMENT: SELF-INTEREST AS POLITICAL CEMENT

A popularly elected regime is likely to reflect more of the social context in which it arises than is a regime that rests primarily on coercion. This is so because the quest for broad popular support entails being responsive to more of the political demands coming from the society. Forging a wide coalition of interests in social contexts that resemble those of the United States at the turn of the century or most new nations today inevitably means developing a capacity to distribute short-run material incentives among potential clients. Few viable political bonds except those of material self-interest are available to build a large political party among poor, heterogeneous, transitional populations. Self-interest thus provides the necessary political cement when neither a traditional governing elite nor a ruling group based on class or ideological interest is available.

Small wonder then, that, faced with the environment we have outlined, parties in the new states have often taken on machine-like traits. This shift frequently has occurred when the symbolic bonds fashioned during the struggle for independence have begun to deteriorate and when what had been a movement confined largely to new urban classes must create a political base for itself among the rest of the population. The decline of broad policy goals and an increasingly narrow concern with the distribution of rewards that maintains a patchwork of interests within the ruling party are the hallmarks of this transformation. The change was most striking in those cases where electoral anxieties were most intense and where the ruling party

[5] For a more detailed analysis of these attitudes and their origin, see Scott, 1968. Chapter 6.

was led by elites without any cohesive ideological vision, e.g., Ceylon, Nigeria, the Philippines,[6] Lebanon, and, increasingly, India. In nations where a single party faces little competition but has not dismantled electoral forms, machine features are often still in evidence.[7]

Among the specific instruments of coordination available to the machine, the power of patronage employment is perhaps the most celebrated. The practice of patronage, however, is by no means confined to modern machine parties—nor is political graft on franchises, contracts, or licenses, for that matter. The ruling party in eighteenth-century England (e.g., the party of Walpole and of Newcastle), operating in a narrow electorate, based its ability to create a viable parliamentary coalition on the distribution of public offices and sinecures to the right people at the right time. Nevertheless, the necessity of generating broad popular support under conditions of universal suffrage has typically meant that modern machine parties wield patronage on a scale that is certainly distinctive.

By exploiting the public purse to provide posts that may be dealt out according to political criteria, the machine party gains a staple means of maintaining internal discipline and cohesion. On the one hand, the diverse groups within the party are linked together by such material rewards as patronage, while on the other, these patronage posts supply the party with a cadre of political workers who are constantly available and who will be responsive to commands from above. It is precisely the diversity of groups having few broad interests in common that renders this pool of available jobs an indispensable basis of organization. The effectiveness of patronage employment as an instrument of coordination hinges, of course, on the kind of clientele I have described—a clientele for whom jobs are of central importance.

The political distribution of patronage was perfected to a fine art by the American urban machine. In the heyday of machines the number of posts dispensed by patronage reached prodigious levels. Around the turn of the century, according to Lincoln Steffens, the Martin machine in Philadelphia had placed 15,000 people in office and "each of these 15,000 persons was selected for office because he could deliver votes, either by organizations, by parties, or by families" (Steffens, 1963, p. 147). This was the case despite the fact that the Philadelphia machine made use of outright electoral fraud as well. In New York City as late as the 1930s, the total annual pay for posts

[6] Because of the powers they exercised within the colonial system and the pattern of early electoral competition, the Philippine parties resembled machines well before independence. The machine pattern of politics in Lebanon is also of longer duration than most.

[7] For single-party states, the significance of material incentives has appeared to grow as the founding leader of the party passed from the scene or as the charisma generated in that period diminished. Communist states in underdeveloped areas are, of course, exceptions.

exempt from civil service regulations—that is, political jobs—exceeded $7 million even after some reforms had been enacted.

While the bastion of patronage in the United States—and hence the bastion of machines—has remained at the state and local levels, federal jobs historically have served to knit together national parties as well. The most striking example may well be Lincoln's victorious Republican Party of 1860 —a hodgepodge of ethnic groups, old Whigs, old Democrats, rural and urban interests, family-based factions, and so forth. Lincoln fully appreciated the importance of "public jobs wisely distributed" as a means of maintaining party unity, and his policies resulted in "the most sweeping removal of federal office holders up to that time in American history."[8] Occupants of roughly twelve hundred of the fifteen hundred posts covered were replaced by the party faithful. As it developed, the distribution of federal jobs not only cemented the party but even may have been largely responsible for containing secessionist pressures in Kentucky, Missouri, Maryland, and Delaware during the Civil War. The political effectiveness of patronage employment was due as much to the importance of federal jobs in the minds of party members who had little else to unite them as to Lincoln's talent for deploying them wisely.

Given the heterogeneous composition of ruling parties in many new nations, the nature of their clienteles, and the scarcity value of government employment, the patronage is, if anything, a more significant adhesive agent than it was in the United States. The "bandwagon effect," whereby the party that won independence grew rapidly in size and eclipsed its rivals, largely resulted from a popular recognition that the party would control the disposal of tangible rewards for some time to come. Conversely, the "negative bandwagon effect" of the disintegration of parties which failed to capture at least a local power base in the early elections was related to the absence of material rewards with which leaders might hold and strengthen their initial following.

Wielding the patronage in new nations, however, occurs in a markedly different legal context than it did in urban America. Saddled with the "very latest" in terms of civil service regulations, politicians in the new nations must regularly resort to practices that are either highly questionable or transparently illegal to find jobs for some party workers. In India, for example, the political career of Pratap Singh Kairon, the Congress Party's Chief Minister of the Punjab, was cut short by a public inquiry that cited him for relatively minor financial peculations and for using his influence to exclude a few posts from normal civil service qualifications.[9] Deprived of open access

[8] Carman and Luthin, 1943, pp. 10, 331. For an account of federal patronage in the first few decades after independence, see Aronson, 1964.

[9] *Report of the Commission of Inquiry into the Matter of Pratap Singh Kairon* ("Das Commission"), 1964, pp. 222, 224, 235. See, for example, the introduction to the *Report of the Committee on Prevention of Corruption* ("Santhanam Report"), 1964; Segal, 1965, Chapter 6; and Dwivedy and Bhargava, 1967.

to the spoils available to party-builders in America or in nineteenth-century England, Kairon was indicted for behavior that would scarcely have raised an eyebrow in Boss Tweed's day. Congress Party politicians, despite the risks, have increasingly made use of the available patronage (not to mention licenses, contracts, franchises) to maintain their electoral strength, secure party cohesion, and even help contain mounting secessionist pressures.

A wide variety of economic measures in new nations merits close analysis for their patronage functions. In this respect, programs of nationalization, while they may answer economic and patriotic needs too, are frequently tailored to maximize the number of patronage posts available to the ruling party. Indonesia prior to Guided Democracy provides a striking example of these mixed motives. When a measure permitting only Indonesian firms to handle sea cargo was implemented, each of the major parties then in the cabinet established its own warehousing firms and simply assumed control of the existing facilities and business. These favored enterprises—although formally within the private sector—supplied a source of income and employment for the ruling parties. Nationalization measures were more successful as a patronage operation than as a means of transferring economic control to Indonesian nationals (Feith, 1962, pp. 478–479.[10]).

Analogous cases from other new nations could be cited at some length, but the Indonesian example is sufficiently illustrative of the general pattern. Patronage pressures are present in military regimes too, but in party-dominated electoral regimes these tendencies arise not only from kinship ties and the desire for wealth, but also from the need to reward party workers and to maintain or broaden popular support.

The party's need to put together a broad coalition is often reflected in structure and operation of development programs as well. Even in Italy, where the ruling (in coalition) Christian Democratic Party depends on votes from the rural south, one expert has written that the Fund for the Development of the South "has become a gigantic *patronage organization* which employs people and awards contracts strictly on the basis of political considerations" (La Palombara, 1964, p. 344; emphasis added). Quite apart from its contribution to economic growth, then, the Fund is managed so as to enhance Christian Democratic electoral strength in the "underdeveloped" south.

Rural development programs in many new nations also are designed with this duality of function in mind. The activities of Malaysia's Ministry of Rural Development, for example, were keyed closely to the electoral re-

[10] See also pp. 366–384 for a more general discussion. The multi-party setting of Indonesia at this time resembled less a strong party machine than a situation in which two or more potential machine parties were vying for power. Patronage and graft, because of the uncertainties, were inevitably more hectic than would have been the case with a stable machine party. The smaller parties, having the fewest long-term concerns and believing that this was their last opportunity, were the most ravenous.

quirements of the Malay branch of the ruling Alliance Party. The employment, "pork-barrel" funds, and contracts generated by its programs were carefully distributed among rural Malays who were deemed assets to the party, and the few areas of solid opposition strength naturally received little or nothing.[11]

The Malaysian and Italian cases each exemplify the effects of particularistic electoral pressures on development schemes. In fact, one would expect to find a greater emphasis placed on extensive rural development programs—programs with a capacity to distribute concrete inducements widely throughout the population—where parties in the new nations must build wide popular support, than where wide support is of only marginal concern. To some extent, *these programs are the functional equivalent of the services American machines performed for first-generation voters in the cities.*

Patronage is but one of the many material incentives available to machine parties. Contract awards, help with the law, selective nonenforcement of taxation, zoning, and safety regulations are, like patronage, part of the bundle of material inducements involving corrupt influence at the enforcement stage that serve as the organizational cement for the typical machine. Where machine pressures are evident in new nations, the development programs pursued are more often amenable to the kind of *political* analysis indicated here than to an analysis which focuses merely on the economic and nationalistic rationale commonly used to justify such programs. The choice among development strategies and the manner of their execution may depend, for the ruling party, less on criteria of growth or productivity than on the level and quality of inducements they place at the party's disposal. If economic success and political payoffs coincide, so much the better. But a project judged a failure by economic planners may nonetheless have achieved precisely the political effects expected of it.[12]

[11] For an example of how the most traditional areas are able to resist machine blandishments, see Nash, 1966, pp. 310–314.

[12] Road-building in Malaysia illustrates this pattern. The present road system is adequate for some time to come and economic planners have thus urged a lower priority for this activity. The almost unique capacity of a large road construction program to reach many rural areas with pork-barrel and patronage employment benefits, however, had led the ruling Alliance Party to continue to pave its way throughout rural Malaysia at much the same rate as in the past. Similar calculations lie behind road programs in other new nations—and in portions of the United States as well.

MACHINE PARTIES IN UNDERDEVELOPED NATIONS

GHANA AND INDIA

8

Having suggested the conditions for the appearance of machine rule and something of its dynamics, we can move to an examination of two political parties whose amply documented activities appear to fit this pattern. Our necessarily brief analysis of Ghana's Convention People's Party (CPP) between 1952 and 1960 and India's Congress Party since shortly after independence will emphasize how each party came to rely on the particularistic distribution of material inducements to maintain and enhance its electoral strength.[1]

GHANA'S CONVENTION PEOPLE'S PARTY (CPP), 1952–1960

Ghana became fully independent only in 1957, but at least by the second CPP electoral victory in 1954, Nkrumah's party was a well established campaign organization with enough control over state finances and decisions to solidify its position. What might be called the "machine era" of the CPP lasted from about 1952 until 1960 when open political competition came to an end. Electoral fraud and coercion were first widely employed during the plebiscite held in 1960 on both a new republican constitution and Nkrumah's presidency. In that year, too, new presidential powers all but eclipsed the legislature and the 1958 Preventive Detention Act was first used to jail a large number of political opponents. After 1960 some machine activity was still in evidence, but it was no longer the mainstay of the regime.

Between 1952 and 1960, however, the dominance of the CPP was increasingly based on machine-style rewards. Coercion, ideology, and charisma were also present as identifiable but minor facets of CPP control. Intimidation was employed during the general elections of 1954 and 1956 and the local elections of 1958, but no one has suggested that such coercive pressures were decisive in the over-all results. Ideological appeals were evident to some degree as well. The CPP's program appealed to many trade union leaders, journalists, school teachers, and school-leavers, while the populist stance of Nkrumah also attracted many young, restless opponents of both traditional chiefs and the privileged Ghanaian colonial elite. Such ideological appeals were based in part on actual expectations of gain and tended to become less important after the CPP gained control over reservoirs of material incentives. Finally, there is little doubt that Nkrumah was a charismatic figure for his people. The only question is how much weight to give to these charismatic bonds. While a definitive answer would require a detailed analysis of Ghanaian public opinion, there is some consensus among experts that the significance of charismatic ties may have been overestimated and that, in any case, there was a steady erosion of ideological

[1] Other instances of electoral machine politics that might well have merited discussion in a lengthier treatment include: The Action Group of Western Nigeria 1954–1964, the party system of Lebanon, Indonesian centrist parties prior to Guided Democracy, the contemporary Philippine political parties, KANU in Kenya until recently, and the AD party in Venezuela for the past five years.

and charismatic authority during this period (Apter, 1968; Zolberg, 1966, p. 145). The concurrent emergence of machine incentives as a major binding force for the CPP was not simply a result of the party's assumption of control over the state; it also reflected the kind of electorate the CPP had to organize and the favorable economic trends that made machine coordination possible.

SOCIAL BASE OF THE CPP

A political machine, as we have noted earlier, prospers best in a milieu where many voters have cast off automatic traditional ties but have not yet developed strong loyalties to modern occupational or class groupings. In this context it is significant that rates of social and economic change in Ghana in the three decades or so before 1950 were among the highest in Africa and provided the CPP with a sizable machine clientele. Ghana at independence had a personal per capita income above $130 per annum, a relatively commercialized agricultural sector buttressed by an extensive trading network and road system, a comparatively high rate of school attendance, and high levels and rates of urbanization.

It was precisely among the mobile young population that the CPP found its most enthusiastic supporters. Looking at the social base of the CPP both in terms of party membership and voting strength in the early period, one finds a high proportion of lower- and lower-middle-class urban dwellers and rural elements detached from the traditional village structures. In particular, the CPP included within its ranks a disproportionate numbers of young urban unemployed ("veranda-boys"), ex-servicemen, school-leavers, school teachers and trade unionists, migrant farmers, market women, and small shopkeepers. Although ideology and charisma played a role in building this support, much of the CPP's social base was more intensely concerned with "jobs, testimonials, contracts, financial help, advice in the courts and so on" (Lewis, 1965, p. 22).

The selective appeal of the CPP is especially striking when it is compared to the social base of its opposition. Whereas the CPP had developed something of a "mass" base, the opposition depended strongly on customary authorities in the northern areas of the country least affected by social change, the privileged class of professionals and civil servants who disdained mass party activity, and a few peripheral minority areas. The main focus of group opposition to the CPP, however, was the large Ashanti area. Here, commercial cocoa farming had taken early root and the structure of customary authority was still quite strong. The Ashanti represented a curious amalgam of traditional deference that resisted machine blandishments and a collective issue-grievance over the low, government-set price of cocoa. Despite some CPP success in exploiting factionalism among the Ashanti, the area's relative solidarity and its new concern with a single broad issue made it a hotbed of opposition. The machine character of the CPP is further underscored by the fact that its support in Ashanti towns came often from the poorer compounds and from non-Ashanti clerks and small shopkeepers (Austin, 1964, p. 314).[2]

It is clear that the CPP's strongest appeal was among the "machine electorate" of young urban migrants, while the opposition found much of its support among the pre-machine, traditional electorate and the old professional elite. Despite the existence of a relatively large machine electorate, however, the CPP had to broaden its base and cultivate a rural clientele in order to win elections. A part of this clientele could be found among the wage laborers, small traders, and dissident village youth (the rural equivalent of the CPP's urban support) and could be attracted by particularistic benefits. Nonetheless, the CPP could not avoid playing tribal politics. It built a rural structure which relied on bribes to chiefs, on tribal animosities, and on pork-barrel benefits for its strength. In contrast to its urban base, then, the rural CPP base was a mixture of new men and traditional leaders who shared a lively appreciation for the personal and group benefits that affiliation with CPP could bring.

INSTRUMENTS OF COORDINATION

The CPP, in the period we are examining, developed an impressive centralized structure for distributing benefits to supporters between and during electoral campaigns. This structure included the coordinated use of government employment patronage; the distribution of contracts, licenses, and individual loans; the use of pork-barrel grants and public works in localities; the centralized collection of kickbacks from large firms with government contracts; and finally the creation of new state corporations for patronage purposes.

Resources In terms of material resources, 1950–1955 was a uniquely favorable period for machine building in Ghana. First, as the CPP assumed the reins of government it gained control over important decisions, local and national budgets, and patronage jobs created by the withdrawal of the British and the expansion of administrative functions. Many joined the CPP in the realization that the party would control the award of licenses, contracts, jobs, loans, and other state-conferred privileges for some time to come. Secondly, the world price of cocoa on which government revenue largely depended rose appreciably on the strength of the

[2] Austin's account is the best and most detailed on the period and I therefore relied heavily on his data and commentary.

Korean War boom, thereby reinforcing the CPP's financial position. Fueled by the resources and prerogatives handed over by the departing colonial power and by favorable economic trends that underwrote expansionary budgets, the CPP became less of a nationalist movement and more of a machine.

Inducements The inducements distributed by the CPP included jobs, contracts, and pork-barrel grants to localities. The pattern of inducements was carefully tailored to each region and sector of the population.

> *The structure of CPP support had been formed in the early and mid-1950's by appealing to local, sectional, and ethnic interests in the countryside, and by building* patronage machines *in the urban areas. The CPP ran main roads through pro-CPP towns instead of through neighboring anti-CPP towns, backed Brongs against Ashantis, and provided ambitious school teachers and petty clerks with well paid quasi-political jobs . . . tactics which won the elections of 1954 and 1956 . . . [Fitch and Oppenheimer, 1966, p. 106].*[3]

The distribution of public jobs was a staple of CPP power. Party cadre clamored for government posts, and such jobs were often given as consolation to CPP activists who failed to win local nomination to an elected post. The threefold growth in Ghana's public budget in this period reflects the pressures on the CPP to provide jobs. Even when cocoa prices plummeted in 1959–1960, indicating that an austerity budget was in order, it was enormously difficult to slow down the rate of growth in public employment, let alone reduce it absolutely. A regime based more on charisma or ideology would perhaps have found it less costly to hold the line on government employment, but for the CPP such a move undermined one of its major bases of support.

The CPP commanded many other material incentives in addition to public-sector jobs. Supporters received preference in bidding for local public works contracts and in applying for agricultural or commercial loans; they were generally shown favoritism at government offices. The opposition, on the other hand, was denied such access and often was overtaxed and harassed for petty violations of the law. The centralized coordination of these rewards and penalties was all but assured by 1956 with the demise of regional assemblies and the creation of district commissioners who were personally responsible to Nkrumah.

[3] This book is an impressive analysis of the CPP which heavily discounts the party's socialist rhetoric.

If the CPP's strength in the towns depended on benefits distributed to individuals and families, its strength in rural areas depended both on winning the favor of traditional leaders and on giving collective pork-barrel benefits to localities. Where chiefs could rely on a deferential following, simple bribery was occasionally sufficient. It was often easier for the CPP to bribe local leaders than to set about creating its own independent following, and by 1956 the rural CPP was based less on young men than on the favor of chiefs who had been amply rewarded. If the chiefs represented a resource to the CPP, the CPP was no less valuable to the chiefs and their followings. In the context of Ghana during the mid-1950s an investment in an opposition candidate was a losing proposition while an investment in a CPP loyalist could be very profitable. The monopoly of the CPP over local development funds, new roads, new schools, and the location of district offices, when coupled with the brokerage expected by voters from their leaders, vastly enhanced the party's attractiveness to customary leaders. If a traditional leader did not declare for the CPP, the voters often backed another pro-CPP claimant who would do more for them as a broker. In brief, then, the CPP relied extensively on material benefits for its support. Its powerful urban base was secured more by the particularistic rewards of the classical urban machine than by ideological or other factors; its weaker rural base rested on a similar strata of restless village youths, on bribes to a number of local chiefs, and on a system of collective pork-barrel rewards to localities that were loyal.

Reward Structures The degree to which Nkrumah and his party managed to centralize and coordinate this system of political patronage is remarkable. The central government and the party provided the basic framework, of course, but development agencies were used as well. Both the Cocoa Purchasing Co. Ltd. (CPC—established in 1952) and NADECO Ltd. (established in 1957) are well-documented cases of the political uses of economic development programs.

The Cocoa Purchasing Co. was established under the Cocoa Marketing Board to organize the buying of cocoa from farmers and to make agricultural loans. As it developed, however, the CPC became a most important financial and patronage tool of the party, especially in the 1954 electoral campaign.[4] The party swelled the CPC staff of buying agents with its own supporters and used the offices, vehicles, and funds of the company as a ready-made rural campaign organization. But the greatest contribution the CPC made to the Convention People's Party—the contribution that prompted a party official to call it the party's "atomic bomb"—was in advancing loans to farmers and to buying agents. Loans, on a vast scale, were given only to those farmers who could prove membership in the pro-CPP United Ghana

[4] Most of the relevant evidence is compiled in the *Report of the Commission of Enquiry into the Affairs of the Cocoa Purchasing Co. Ltd.* ("Jibowu Commission"), 1956.

Farmers' Council (UGFC). The tempo of loan activity reached a peak in the six weeks prior to the 1954 election as the party guaranteed itself a solid majority.

Since the CPC became primarily a political instrument rather than an economic means to organize the cocoa trade, its performance as a public business enterprise was deplorable. Loans were made to the most loyal farmers, not to the most efficient. The political nature of the loans made it impossible to prosecute defaulters, and unpaid debts accumulated rapidly. Given the patronage basis of CPC employment, there was also a great deal of petty corruption within the organization. In brief, the activities which made the CPC an effective instrument of machine politics made it, at the same time, an economic fiasco.

While the function of the CPC had been largely to distribute incentives to rural voters, the function of NADECO Ltd.—established in 1957, five months after the abolition of the CPC—was to fulfill the other machine function of providing money for the ruling party. NADECO functioned as the party's collection agency for bribes paid by western European companies and Ghanaian contractors who were awarded government contracts; it quickly became the single most significant source of purely party funds. The "informal commission" paid to NADECO was between 5 and 10 percent of the contract amount, and suppliers understood that payment of this commission was part of the cost of continuing to do business with Ghana (Report of the Commission [of Enquiry into NADECO Ltd.] . . . , 1966, p. 44). For large purchases of such items as government busses, automobiles, airplanes, and locomotives the amount was substantial. The effect of this system was to create, in nominally socialist Ghana, a network of politically oriented capitalist enterprises under the protective wing of the CPP. Most such firms naturally figured the cost of bribes into the contract price or else recouped the loss by supplying inferior materials or otherwise violating contract terms. Ultimately it was the Ghanaian taxpayer—especially the cocoa farmer—who paid the cost of these bribes via official government revenue with which the contracting firms were paid.

What was striking about NADECO was not the fact that foreign firms paid kickbacks on contracts, but rather the extent to which the CPP centralized the process of bribe-collection that in other nations occurs in a much more decentralized, *ad hoc* fashion. The party's control over all government financial and development decisions was thus used to provide a regular and predictable source of direct income for the party. Prior to 1960 at least, most of the proceeds from NADECO were invested in maintaining the CPP's electoral machine throughout the country.[5]

[5] From 1957 through 1965, NADECO received £1,697,030, largely in bribe payments, of which at least £588,000 was *visibly* transferred to CPP accounts. Nkrumah disposed of much of the remainder, both personally, in the form of private grants and favors, and in his capacity as head of the CPP. *Report of the Commission* [of Enquiry into NADECO Ltd.] . . . , 1966, pp. 16, 23, *et seq.*

ECONOMIC POLICY AND MACHINE POLITICS

For the 1953–1960 period, the efforts to nationalize sectors of the economy and to begin the creation of a socialist state can be fully understood only against the background of machine politics. The creation of the CPC, for example, had the avowed purpose of breaking the hold of private sector middlemen and money lenders over the cocoa trade. But the CPC was valuable for other reasons. It centralized much public patronage in the party's hands while providing a large cash reserve for use in electoral struggles. Thus the goals of reorganizing and centralizing the cocoa trade corresponded closely with the desire of CPP leaders to maximize the political utility of government employment and expenditure.

Mixed motives were at work in many of the economic and administrative changes initiated during this period. To mention a few, the Housing Corporation, the Ghana National Construction Co., the Industrial Development Corporation, the centralization of the banking system, the growing socialization of retail trade and control of import-export business—all of these enterprises and policy choices were in keeping with the doctrinal goals of nationalization and socialism. On the face of it, any socialist-inclined ruling party would have followed much the same course in organizing and planning its economy. The explanatory power of ideology, however, is of much less use when it comes to accounting for either the day-to-day operation of these enterprises or the actual implementation of broad policies. Here we encounter the distribution of housing for patronage purposes, the paramount role of political calculations in the location of government public works and state industries, the informal use of bank overdrafts to finance the party, and the "shaking down" of contractors and merchants for campaign funds in return for favored treatment. Doctrinal beliefs do not explain this behavior; it must be seen as a response to the political needs of a ruling party. For the period we are examining, the actual economic policy of the CPP can be more successfully viewed as a response to pressures of machine politics than as simply a matter of ideologically motivated decisions.

THE DECLINE OF MACHINE POLITICS

A machine party, as we have noted, mobilizes its support on the basis of its capacity to deliver material rewards to individuals, families, small groups, and even village units. As such, its control is threatened by the emergence of broad policy demands or by a decline in the material resources at its disposal.

It was just such a combination of events which brought the "machine era" of the CPP to an end in Ghana. First, the export price of cocoa declined precipitously in 1960, thereby jeopardizing the main foundation of expansionary budgets and large-scale imports. In an effort to maintain high budget levels, Ghana for the first time sought foreign loans as her reserves dwindled and the consumer price index edged upward. The CPP was losing its financial sinews at a time when the party depended increasingly on material rather than symbolic bonds for its cohesiveness.

The contraction of the economy itself exacerbated latent collective demands within Ghana. In an effort to raise revenue, or at least to minimize losses, the government was paying cocoa producers less in 1960 than at any time in the past decade, thereby reinforcing opposition to the CPP, particularly in the Ashanti areas. Government white-collar and blue-collar employees, for their part, were increasingly restive as their real incomes were eroded by inflation. This restiveness took the form of strikes among unionized workers who resented new deductions from their paychecks and repudiated their CPP-affiliated leadership.

Simply because of the structural changes in the economy, collective demands were now more explosive than they would have been five years before. The socialization of the economy meant that many demands for higher wages or crop prices—demands that previously would have been directed at private-sector firms—were now transformed into direct confrontations with the government. When the government has become a major employer it can no longer act as a disinterested arbiter in labor disputes; such disputes unavoidably involve a direct challenge to the ruling party.

What we are suggesting here is that in 1960–1961 the pattern of machine politics could no longer be sustained. The resources at the disposal of the party had dwindled, collective economic issues were becoming more severe and unmanageable, and there is even some doubt as to whether the CPP could have won an open election in this atmosphere of austerity. Before 1960 the fiscal health of Ghana had allowed *both* capital development and the large expenditures necessary to fuel the CPP electoral machine. By 1960 these twin goals could not be sustained simultaneously. The CPP could hope to remain an electoral regime only by meeting demands that would foreclose any capital development. Capital development, on the other hand, could occur only at the cost of abandoning expensive competitive electoral forms and relying more on coercion. Nkrumah was clearly inclined to the authoritarian solution which would allow him to pursue his vision for Ghana. The main point, however, is that a choice was required. The full costs of machine politics had become evident in the context of economic crisis and burgeoning collective demands that undermined the machine party's capacity to control the situation.

THE INDIAN NATIONAL CONGRESS UNTIL 1969

Founded in 1855, the Indian National Congress is older than most parties in the west. Only after independence in 1947, however, did the party turn in earnest to the task of building an electoral apparatus. Given the enormous size, population, and variety of social structures within India, we can scarcely attempt a thorough description of the party's evolution; instead, at the risk of some oversimplification, we will confine ourselves to an analysis of major trends.[6]

As the "movement" qualities of the Congress Party faded after 1947, the leadership, both locally and nationally, turned increasingly to machine-style incentives to retain electoral majorities. Newly won control over patronage, licensing, and state loans provided, as it had in Ghana, the raw material for forging new alliances. But unlike the situation in Ghana, machine resources were relatively slender and control over them never became sufficiently centralized to permit the creation of a strong nationwide Congress machine. What developed instead was an assemblage of state and local Congress Party organizations which relied heavily on short-run material incentives; in a few areas a concentration of resources and leadership created a fairly cohesive machine pattern, while in many other areas the fragmentation of power and resources resulted in a much more anarchic or feudal pattern.[7]

GROWTH OF MACHINE PRESSURES

Once the Congress Party became the ruling party of an independent India, new forces were set in motion which transformed it. First, and most obvious,

[6] Although what follows is a description of electoral-based patronage and corruption, it should be emphasized that a great deal of purely bureaucratic or administrative corruption is to be found in India—as in Ghana. Landlords and businessmen, for example, have made use of their contacts with administrators (as well as with politicians) to change the implementation of policy at the enforcement stage. For evidence of this, see *Report of the Railway Corruption Enquiry Committee*, 1955; or *Report of the Committee on Prevention of Corruption*, 1964, for details. There is strong evidence that the Indian public assumes, probably with good reasons, that administrative corruption is widespread. Well over half of respondents to a survey felt that 50 percent or more of government officials were corrupt. Cf. Eldersveld *et al.*, 1968, p. 29. The dominant position of the Congress Party, however, has made it an increasing focus for influencing policy implementation. Those administrators who were previously free-lance brokers are more commonly now acting according to party wishes.

This account is based on an analysis of the National Congress before its split into two entities; the New Congress led by Indira Ghandi that is somewhat less machine-like than its parent, and the Old Congress led by "the Syndicate" which is a strikingly machine-like coalition of regional bosses.

[7] It should be understood that, given India's vast size and population, a statewide machine there might involve ten times the population and five times the area of the entire nation of Ghana. Thus a statewide Indian machine is of nation-state proportions.

the goals of the party changed. As a nationalist movement the party had needed and attracted charismatic leaders and ideological adherents. As a ruling party, Congress acquired a broader electoral base and an influx of more prosaic politicians who, although they might still inspire patriotism, tended to be more adept at administering party affairs and winning electoral struggles than at staging mass protests.

In another sense the change in local Congress leadership was a reflection of its new resources. Like most other new ruling parties, the Congress Party was faced with the task of digesting a host of new adherents who were attracted by its control over the state. Unlike Ghana's CPP, however, Congress's party funds and patronage employment were relatively meager and the party had somewhat less than total influence on the conduct of administration. This meant that supporters were attracted to it more by the chances it offered for nominations to office and for legal *access* to decision-makers within the administration who made license, permit, quota, and loan decisions, than by the direct goods or employment Congress could distribute.

A natural bandwagon effect changed the social base of the party as local leaders, traders, shopkeepers, landlords, and many others who saw the potential advantages of political influence flocked to its banner. The importance of access grew steadily as the public sector of the economy expanded and as administrative decisions were increasingly politicized. On the one hand, the new adherents were welcomed as additions to the party's electoral strength amidst a widened suffrage. On the other hand, these new allies represented a more opportunistic clientele; they were tied to the party and its local leaders largely by the flow of material benefits. Their affiliation to the party thus promoted the rise of machine-style local leadership adept at sustaining a coalition based on narrow and concrete interests. Compared to preindependence leaders and followers, the newcomers were conspicuous for their indifference to broad ideological issues but intensely moved by the distribution of loaves and fishes. Once having captured the governmental apparatus, the bonds of ideology and broad policy loosened and networks of material rewards became more pervasive. As this occurred, the "ideological following" of Congress, especially among the intelligentsia, was lost, either to left-wing parties or to passive alienation.

The importance of administrative access to Congress adherents is highlighted by the party's decision to base its organization on administrative districts even when these districts did not coincide with constituency units. This choice was made in recognition of the party's dependence on influence at the enforcement stage in local units of administration. Help with public employment, scholarships, contracts, permits, loans, and the filing of various applications is the key to party strength in the districts and this help can be most easily provided by making the party units coincide with administrative units.

THE MATERIAL BASIS OF LEADERSHIP

To speak of political competition before the mid-1960s in India was largely to speak of competition *within* the Congress Party. Until then, the Congress dominated most state governments, so that much of the potential opposition remained within the party in the hopes of improving their position rather taking the great risk of leaving. As material bonds became steadily more important, internal Congress politics became largely a contest between factions for access to the most rewarding opportunities. The party's central leadership, unlike Nkrumah, lacked the concentration of resources that would have allowed it to reduce factional battles.

The basis of most sizable political factions in India—once one moves beyond a small core of close friends and relatives, or traditional village cleavages—is the quest for quick material payoffs. This is true not only of many active adherents of the faction but of its passive voting support as well. Efforts by politicians to create broad organizational support have usually failed, "because the ordinary voter has an extremely narrow range of public responsibility and is not willing to give time and effort without the promise of immediate material reward. . . . Parties have no moral appeal" (Bailey, 1963, p. 135). A potential candidate starts out with a nucleus of supporters tied to him by caste, community, or kinship loyalties, but most of his following remains loyal by virtue of the "favors and services done or promised" them (Brass, 1965, p. 164). Without either private resources or access to the public resources of government to sustain a following, a faction tends to disintegrate as its members seek other connections.[8] It is because factions within Congress were fueled by patronage and money that much conflict swirled around state or local bastions of patronage such as district and municipal boards, cooperatives, and local banks.

The best indicators of the material basis of Congress Party politics were the host of local "middlemen"—also called "expeditors" or "brokers"—who linked the rank and file of the party to the higher echelons of government. Their various activities can best be differentiated using the three main categories of local administrative functions: regulation, extraction, and dis-

[8] Weiner, 1967, p. 257. In basic structure, such factions are not too dissimilar from elite cliques in Thailand. The difference, however, is that they are pervasive at the village level in India, where one must create an *electoral* following. The factions are thus much larger, extend further down the social pyramid, and are often based, in the village, on more permanent cleavages such as caste or family feuds of long duration. Weiner not only explicitly treats Congress as a machine but also provides an unequaled wealth of comparable case studies of individual districts. I lean heavily on his descriptions and analysis here, although I am much more pessimistic than he about the stability of its machine coordination and find its effects much more profoundly conservative in terms of the inability of the party to avoid being swallowed up by its basically reactionary social base.

tribution.[9] In the regulatory area a local Congress official helped people in trouble with the law, assisted in procuring permits and licenses for small businesses, or helped in obtaining a favorable administrative decision for a constituent on such matters as land titles, debts, and so forth. In the area of extraction—taxation largely—the party broker assisted in gaining an adjustment of taxes for his clients, or perhaps helped them avoid some taxes altogether. Finally, and most important, the local expeditor was the central figure in the distribution of government goods and services to the locality. Here the broker provided selective access to agricultural loans, scholarships and places in schools and universities, patronage employment, hospital treatment, fertilizers, and help generally in filling out government forms and approaching the administration for such benefits.

One may distinguish the resource base of factions in Congress according to their dependence on private or public resources. In some areas landlords and merchants employed their personal wealth and control to create a following that is relatively independent of the government. Elsewhere factions rested largely on brokerage or access to local or district public bodies, in which case the degree of coruption was likely to be greater. In practice, however, one was likely to find factions whose leaders had some private resources but depended on influence over official patronage for a substantial part of their following.

The Congress organization in most states was a vertical chain of the factional alliances we have described. Local village factions competed to gain influence with dominant district and state factions so as to receive enough resources to maintain and expand their local strength. State-level factions, for their part, sought connections with strong local factions in order to improve their chance of controlling the state party and winning statewide elections. The *ad hoc* alliance system thereby created involved local factions delivering votes to their statewide factional allies in return for whatever patronage and favors the larger unit could supply to its local affiliates. Ties between factions at each level were subject to continual reassessment, for while local factions often grew out of enduring social cleavages in the local environment, their affiliation to outside factions was generally based on calculating the material advantages involved.

The inability of Congress to substantially moderate factional strife was due both to the local social structure it faced and to its conscious policy of decentralizing development. First, it faced a number of local leaders whose wealth, landholdings, or traditional status gave them an independent base of power. Second, and most important, the community development programs and local councils (*panchayati*) have created a host

[9] This is the classification used by Weiner, 1967, p. 257, and by Almond and Powell, 1967, *passim.*

of local centers of patronage and favor that could seldom be controlled by state party leaders. These local organizations, which were set up partly for ideological and partly for electoral reasons, provided local faction leaders with a base of power that allowed them to drive hard bargains with higher party bosses or even to defy the wishes of the larger party. In a sense, Congress has traded a short-term gain in electoral strength for a substantial reduction in its capacity for central coordination.

CONGRESS' RURAL MACHINE: TAKEOVER FROM BELOW

No Urban Machines India, unlike the United States, has not been characterized by the growth of urban machines. Although machine characteristics are evident in urban politics, local machine regimes have failed to develop despite the existence in most cities of many migrants and recently enfranchised voters, of desperately poor citizens for whom small favors might be welcome, and of business interests which can profit by influencing the administration.

However, a number of other preconditions for the development of urban machines are lacking. First, the city is generally dwarfed by the state as the locus of the financial and decision-making powers that a machine needs to control. Most of the material rewards and decisions involving Calcutta, for example, are in the hands of the West Bengal State government rather than the Calcutta Municipal Council.[10] Secondly, in the larger cities, Congress already faces the growth of militant left-wing opposition from sectors of the middle class and the poor who are motivated by collective goals and buttressed organizationally by trade unions. Increasing reliance on repression of opposition by the police and by preventive detention, and on the prohibition of public assemblies may indicate that much of the population is no longer manipulable by machine-style inducements.[11]

Democracy and Ruralization In the course of organizing to win elections in the states and for the national parliament, the Congress party had of necessity relied increasingly on India's main reservoir of voters: the rural population. Looking at the development of the party since independence, one notes on the one hand, a fairly steady erosion of

[10] For a discussion of Calcutta politics, cf. Weiner, 1967, Chaps. 16, 17, pp. 321–170; Franda, 1966, pp. 420–433; and the *Report of the Corporation of Calcutta Enquiry Commission* ("Talukder Committee Report"), Calcutta: 1962, *passim.*

[11] Given the fact that resources are also lacking, it is difficult to determine whether a sizable machine-workable electorate is lacking or simply the resources to "work" it. Congress does, however, rely heavily on urban business interests for campaign contributions, in return for which it assists them in organizing access to state and national decision-makers.

Congress strength in the cities, and on the other a steady improvement in the influence of rural, state, and district bosses within the party. In this process Congress was transformed from a rather narrow bourgeois nationalist movement led primarily by westernized elites into a more broadly based coalition that was both more rural and, one might even say, more indigenous.

The ruralization of Congress was largely a consequence of electoral necessity. With the rapid expansion of suffrage, Congress faced the same dilemma which has confronted elected nationalist parties in many new nations: how to absorb vast numbers of new political participants while at the same time preserving the goals and cohesion of the movement. In its starkest form the question was whether Congress could assimilate the new social base or whether the new social base would simply overwhelm and destroy the party.

For the party to have transformed and assimilated its new social base, it would have needed the power and cohesiveness to break down the strong structures of allegiance in the countryside. If the party had been more ideologically unified, if it had had the capacity to create its own rural cadre committed to party goals, and if there had been a greater concentration of power and resources at the center, it might have been equal to this staggering task. As none of these conditions was met, the social base tended to triumph over the party at the local level despite the fact that Congress did not face serious electoral difficulties for some time after independence. In the districts Congress was forced to deal with the electorate through its existing patron-brokers who, as landowners and caste-leaders, had no desire to jeopardize their positions by transforming local social structures. In adapting to local conditions, the party thus increasingly became tied to age-old patterns of status and leadership. The basic process is aptly described by one theorist of political development.

> *The tendency for landed elements to dominate the legislature in modernizing societies with electoral competition reflects the absence of effective political organizations. The bulk of the population is in the countryside, and hence the nature of the regime is determined by the nature of the electoral process in the countryside. In the absence of effective parties, peasant unions or other political organizations, the crucial resources are economic wealth and social status, and the traditional elites capitalize upon their possession of these to secure election . . . [Huntington, 1968, p. 390].*

Some important changes, of course, did occur. Numerically strong castes often fared better as a result of their new electoral muscle. Traditional leaders, now having to compete for votes, had to rely on palpable material inducements as well as on deference to mobilize and strengthen their followings. In addition, the development of a stratum of political brokers (who often enjoyed high traditional status as well) around the new local programs and elective bodies provided a new channel of upward mobility. Finally, the leadership of local princes and huge landowners tended to yield to a second rung of prosperous peasant proprietors. The pressure to win elections, however, impelled Congress to validate and bolster the authority of whatever local leaders were available. In areas where commercialization and social change had gone furthest this meant adapting to new landed proprietors and more mobile new elites. In areas where customary authority was still strong it meant adapting to traditional caste leaders and landowners—even to princes in some regions.

In electoral terms the ruralization of Congress may have been a rational policy choice. Not only was the bulk of the population there, but a strong case can be made that the mobilization of rural votes is less costly—in a financial sense—than the mobilization of urban votes. Rural voters are more often motivated by deference than urban voters; thus securing the support of a rural leader will bring more voters to the party at less cost than coopting an urban leader whose following demands more material rewards. Also, the fact that rural voters are grouped in village units permits the use of collective pork-barrel inducements such as wells, schools, and roads, whereas wooing the urban vote requires a more particularistic and usually more costly strategy. Finally, urban voters are likely to have higher aspirations and demands, making it more expensive to mobilize them. The ease with which the Congress could use local social structure to reach village voters thus lowered the organizational and financial costs of mobilizing the electorate, while at the same time changing the very nature of the party.

Leadership changes within the party since independence reflect the price Congress has paid; "top positions in the government and the party came to be occupied by a new group of leaders who had come up through the local and state Congress structures and who were particularly responsive to local, communal, and rural demands rather than to national ones" (Huntington, 1968, p. 446). The vast rural machine constructed by the party's use of patronage, pork-barrel grants, and community development did serve to temper and dilute the strength of some communal-linguistic demands. On the whole, however, local social structure tended to dominate the Congress.

Conservatism Regardless of whether Congress' local base came to rest on traditional leaders or on those who had moved up during the colonial economic transformation, it is fair to say that the dynamics of electoral competition made the party more conservative as well as more locally-rooted. As the party incorporated powerful local leaders with ready-made followings in order to win elections it tended to lose its ideologically motivated party workers to left-wing competitors.[12] Unable to trans-

[12] For a detailed account of the changing composition of the Congress Party elite in one state, see Bailey, 1963, pp. 196–215.

form rural society, Congress became more representative of conservative rural elites. These elites were hardly inclined to favor any radical agrarian measures which would challenge their position; what is more, their bargaining strength within the party was often reinforced by their relative autonomy. The pace of "conservatization" was most rapid in those areas where the party's majority was most tenuous. Where the party was strongest it could afford to "starve" out dissident factions, but where it was weak it had to come to terms with as many dissidents as possible. "Coming to terms" in most cases meant having a state Congress whose policy goals were largely confined to a distribution of spoils.

Creating a vast rural electoral base in a comparatively short time moved Congress unavoidably toward the protection of the agrarian status quo. Its success as an integrative party bridging the gap between cities and countryside, between different castes, and between ethnic/linguistic groups had been achieved at great cost. Returning to our earlier distinction between parties that transform and assimilate new clienteles and parties that are overrun and transformed *by* their new membership, it is fairly clear that the Congress party largely fell victim to its new supporters. As one observer of district politics notes, "It is not that Congress has taken control of the district, but that those who had control of the district have taken over Congress" (Weiner, 1967, p. 234). The bargain had been struck mostly on the terms of this rural elite and not on the terms of the party's leadership. As a result Congress' program for change in 1965 was but a pale reflection of its aspirations for change in 1948.

Feudalization The growing conservatism of the Congress Party had been greatly facilitated by the far-reaching decentralization of political decisions and development programs. Partly because of Ghandian doctrine and partly because of Congress' growing reliance on rural votes, a host of local institutions with financial and patronage powers had been created to serve as power bases for local elites. Not only was Congress' authority diluted by reliance on rural elites with private resources of wealth and status; it was also diluted by the growth of a local class of politicians with entrenched access to public resources.

Given the increasing patronage basis of Congress organization and the creation of local cooperative and development institutions, it follows that the capture of these local institutions was the focus of district politics. This multiplicity of local control centers introduced a certain democratization of development and expanded opportunities for local political participation. At the same time, it also contributed to a feudalization of the party in which factions that captured some of these local patronage bodies could defy party discipline. Having a reasonably secure source of material rewards, a dominant local faction could demand a high price for cooperation. As in any highly decentralized system, this feudal pattern had a certain stability; even if Congress lost assembly seats at the state level, it could retain many nuclei of strength in the districts. Such stability was attained, however, at an enormous cost in factionalism accompanied by a loss of capacity for concerted action.

Thus a major reason why India has machine-style politics without a cohesive machine is this transfer of control of material inducements to the local level. Where there is centralization of the material basis of coordination, as in Ghana, the party can make more demands on its following, reward loyalty and punish defection, gain acceptance of policy demands, and generally bargain with local branches from a position of strength. Where, on the other hand, material incentives are distributed by locally controlled institutions, as in India, one may expect a fragmented machine party with a sharply reduced capacity for coordinated action—machine-style politics without a machine, or, at best, local machines which form the basis of state and national factions. Under these circumstances a feudal pattern develops in which the party can make few demands on its following, cannot punish recalcitrant units, cannot forge an agreed upon set of policy goals, and is generally at the mercy of its local branches when it comes to bargaining. The decentralization of development and authority in India helped foster a cacophony of entrenched factions (based on traditional leadership and/or local patronage) and local machines that could not be knit into a cohesive national party.[13]

DISTRIBUTION AND WELFARE VERSUS PRODUCTION

A machine-style governing party builds an electoral coalition largely on the basis of concrete material inducements (patronage, access, favors, pork-barrel, etc.) which it distributes among the electorate. It is concerned far more with measures of distribution and welfare than with production or structural change. In this context, Congress' rural program emphasized the demands of its clientele. Roads, wells, agricultural loans, schools, community halls, and more particularistic favors and patronage were the primary instruments of Congress' hold in rural areas. These activities not only won votes, they also accorded nicely with the party's conception of socialism as primarily welfare and distribution (Weiner, 1967, pp. 464, 473). Congress did much better at expanding government expenditure and employment than it did at expanding India's rate of economic growth. What the party did not do well—or, more accurately, seldom attempted—was to transform the basic structure of rural society, to create loyalty to broad policy goals, to push hard for substantial changes in agricultural techniques, or to make political sacrifices for production goals.

[13] Although he is generally much more optimistic than I believe the record warrants, Weiner (1967, p. 482) expresses the same dilemma: "It can and has been argued that a party which adapts itself well to a rural, traditional society cannot readily change that society."

The reasons for the party's lopsided capacities are obvious. As a political organization, Congress' short-run future depended on keeping the material rewards flowing at a steady or increasing rate; any cutback in distributive and welfare programs would threaten it with disintegration. In addition, the actual form and location of capital expenditures which were made in the countryside (where the votes are, but where the capital/output ratio is less favorable) were increasingly dependent on political rather than production considerations. The road that brought in more votes was more likely to be built than the road that generated more economic activity. The loss of reformist zeal also was explained by the party's organization, for Congress' local structure depended on locally dominant landholding groups whose future would generally have been imperiled by any radical program of agrarian transformation. It is not so much that Congress was actively reactionary as that it built an organization on whatever local structures were available, and it was thus unable to jeopardize the existing basis of rural leadership.

The relative emphasis on distribution versus production and reform shifted at different levels of the government and party. National party leaders and bureaucrats were more likely to be concerned with goals of structural change, but the lower we move in the party hierarchy, the greater became the concern with distribution and consumption. In this sense the gradual decentralization and ruralization of the government placed greater power in the hands of those who were least concerned with development and production. This tension was symbolized, to a great extent, in Mrs. Ghandi's efforts in 1969 to wrest control of the party from "The Syndicate" of conservative leaders who had by then come to dominate much of the party apparatus in the states.

Finally, there is good cause to suspect that this problem became more acute over time for the original Congress Party. The increasing electoral weakness of the Congress Party created new pressures for more distributive measures in at least two respects. First, a weakened party was less able to resist material demands from district and local factions whose defection lost them a statewide election. When the party was clearly dominant it could afford to ignore groups whose demands threatened its national program, but when it was fighting for its life it opened itself to extortion by many of these same districts. In close elections the bargaining power of holdouts is greatly inflated. Second, Congress' electoral weakness led to an even greater devolution of authority to the local level. The price for cooperation among factions was not only more material benefits, but also more local control over their distribution. Thus a decline in production goals was accompanied by a decline in the power of the center to set and enforce any goals at all. Having adapted so successfully to the pattern of India's segmented rural social structure to win elections, the Congress party found itself increasingly a prisoner of that social structure. So long as the fundamental problems of structural change and productivity remained, they gradually created a kind of long-term social dynamite that threatened the entire Congress structure.

Alienated from the stagnation characteristic of the "Old Congress," the New Congress of Indira Ghandi brought together those who still cherished the original Congress' vision of social transformation and many others who felt that the days of the Syndicate were numbered. The success of the New Congress at the polls, however, highlighted the dilemmas of electoral politics in India; in order to gather a winning coalition, the group around Indira Ghandi had to come to terms with many state factions which threatened its long-run capacity to carry through basic structural changes.

CONCLUSIONS

The cases of Ghana's Convention People's Party (CPP) and India's Congress Party reveal the strength of the pressures that lead a nationalist party after independence to rely on concrete material inducements when it must win majorities in a still largely traditional countryside. Both parties relied increasingly on machine-style inducements to maintain their majorities as opposition developed and as the symbolic bonds of the nationalist period eroded. In each instance the expansion of government activity—more public employees, a growing public investment program, increasing economic regulations, community development schemes—was instrumental in propelling and structuring the distribution of machine blandishments.

There were important differences between the patterns of machine politics in each country. While Congress was considerably more rural-based, the CPP depended more on support from urban areas and from rural areas where customary authority had eroded. Because it could therefore deal more particularistically with voters the CPP was somewhat less burdened with traditional local structures than was the Congress Party. As a result, the CPP had a clientele that, although it may have demanded more material benefits and thus created more corruption, was more receptive to party leadership and to far-reaching policy initiatives. In terms of the mix of inducements, Congress found pork-barrel programs especially useful as collective rewards for its more traditional following. The CPP, on the other hand, "worked" its disaggregated following more by individual favors, bribes, and patronage.

Perhaps the biggest difference between the Congress' brand of machine politics and that of the CPP, however, is the CPP's much greater centralization of control over the material resources of politics. The CPP was able to use its banks, cocoa marketing institutions, and development programs as instruments of centralized coordination that allowed it to punish enemies, reward followers, and thus create a disciplined party. In short, the CPP coordinated the distribution of machine-style rewards to build a political machine. India's Congress party, by contrast, had so dispersed control over machine-type rewards that the development of a national machine was, under the circumstances, inconceivable. The very dispersal of Congress power may have made it more stable than the CPP, inasmuch as it was therefore more firmly rooted in the social structure, so that a single election could not sweep away its basis of power. Thus Congress's decentralization lent its regime some stability at the cost of an immobility on policy, whereas the CPP's centralization achieved policy flexibility at the cost of regime instability.

The CPP and Congress depended increasingly on concrete material rewards to build their electoral coalition. As one would expect, they were especially vulnerable to demands which were not amenable to those rewards. Such demands may come from the old order—e.g., form traditional groupings with linguistic, religious, and other parochial demands—or they may come from a newer order—e.g., from trade unions, business groups, or peasant associations with more class-based policy demands. The potential challenges to machine parties from both older loyalties and newer loyalties thus reflect the transitional character of machine-style politics. In India, those members of the Congress Party who were more committed to structural change tended to join the New Congress faction under Indira Ghandi's leadership. Second, machine parties are especially vulnerable to a decline in the pool of rewards at their disposal. This threat is more immediate in centralized regimes like Ghana's and slower-acting in decentralized India. Any economic setback that decreases government revenue is in both instances a direct threat to the viability of the material links between the party and its following. Finally, the inevitable by-products of machine politics may alienate key elites who are in a position to challenge the regime.[14] The corruption, bribery, and opportunism fostered by the machine, its weakness as an instrument of social transformation, its emphasis on distributive policies over long-run growth may be important factors here. In the next chapter we shall analyze more carefully the reasons for the collapse of political machines.

[14] Or, as in Ghana's case the party leader himself may decide to transform the character of the regime.

THE MACHINE

AN OLIGARCHIC RESPONSE TO DEMOCRATIC PRESSURES

9

The growth of machine-style politics often represents a large-scale effort by elite groups to manage the problem of rapidly expanding political participation while at the same time retaining their control over state policy. No such effort was required in early Stuart England or twentieth-century Thailand, where participation was confined to a narrow stratum of the population. In this limited sense, machine politics signifies the democratization of certain forms of corruption; the number of participants has increased, the distribution of rewards must be more extensive, and a more elaborate organizational and financial base is required. Just as in the realm of political violence the shift from palace coups to internal war represents an escalation in participation, so in the realm of corruption the shift from aristocratic-elite-centered venality to machine politics represents an escalation in participation.

A CONSERVATIVE RESPONSE TO CHANGE

Thriving in periods of rapid social change and expanding suffrage, machine-style politics nevertheless represents a conservative response to its dynamic environment.[1] Machine politics is conservative in at least these four respects: (1) it represents an alternative to violence in managing conflict; (2) it may well increase the legitimacy of a regime for "transitional" populations; (3) it emphasizes short-run particularistic gains at the expense of broad, long-run transformations; (4) it avoids class issues and fosters interclass collaboration.

It is crucial to specify here that although these effects may flow in part from corrupt practices, they are attributable to machine politics and not to corruption *per se*. The central fact about a political machine is that it aims at the "political consolidation of the beneficiaries" of the patronage and graft system for electoral ends (Key, 1936, p. 394). Whereas nonmachine corruption more often involves purely personal competition for spoils or aims only at the consolidation of narrow elites who control wealth or armed force, the machine must remain popular to survive and consequently must meet demands from a broader stratum of citizens. Not all corruption is machine politics and not all machine politics is corrupt.

AVOIDING VIOLENCE

The social setting of the machine is ordinarily one where ties to the community as a whole are weak and where the potential for violence is great. The capacity of the machine to organize and provide material inducements (often corruptly) operates as a means of solving, for the time being at least, conflicts of interest that might otherwise generate violence. In order to re-

[1] The use of the term "conservative" here is not entirely satisfactory in covering the effects described. In any event, each of the separate effects may be considered individually.

main popular and thereby win elections, the machine must continually make a place for new, ambitious leaders who could potentially threaten its control. By coopting new leaders, the machine is responsive to particularistic new demands while simultaneously safeguarding its own future.

Much of the corruption for which big-city machines in the United States were noted represented an informal integration of demands which the formal political system all but excluded from consideration. In return for their support of the machine boss, the newly arrived European immigrants received patronage employment, special attention in court, and loans and welfare payments which were often outside the bounds of strict legality. For most immigrants, the machine's connections, knowledge of the ropes, and *promise* of help in time of need was as effective as the delivery of concrete rewards. Thus groups which might otherwise have become susceptible to more radical, not to say revolutionary, doctrines were effectively domesticated and given a stake in the system. Much the same might be said of electoral regimes in many new nations: the villagers who have recently arrived in the cities, the businessmen and shopkeepers from insecure minority groups, have all been attached, in greater or lesser degree, to the informal political system which attempts to meet their needs and demands. Corruption acts on such groups essentially as a conservative force which, by granting many of them concrete rewards, weds them more firmly to the political system and dilutes the impulse toward more radical solutions.

In some settings, then, it may be appropriate to view machine corruption as a sort of half-way house between violence and constitutionality—a means by which some of the demands generated by a vast increase in political participation are nonviolently accommodated within a political system whose formal institutions are as yet inadequate to the task. By increasing the government's *de facto* capacity to meet certain demands and by reducing the likelihood of political violence, the corruption that accompanies machine politics may contribute to the stability both of a particular regime and of the electoral system itself.

The tangible rewards of the machine can also, for a time at least, retard the development of vehement demands for large-scale reforms transcending particularistic interests. A striking example of this is the 1946 presidential election in the Philippines where machine inducements were used to temporarily defuse an economic system highly charged with a potential for violence. Faced with a "rising tide of peasant labor discontent," the main sugar, banking, and commercial interests contributed enormous funds to the Liberals, whose electoral campaign virtually smothered the revolutionary fires with cash (Baterina, 1955, p. 81).

The Philippine case illustrates the *limits* of machine conciliation as well. While developing a great capacity for coopting new leaders and distributing particularistic incentives, parties in the Philippines have been unable either to carry out reforms of the agrarian structure or to meet emerging class or broad policy demands. Consequently the party system lurches from election to election with each side patching together a temporary winning coalition on the basis of patronage, bribes, and pork-barrel. The pattern of net government operating receipts for the past decade shows consistent and increasingly severe deficits in the months before an election as the ruling party deploys all the financial resources it can muster to win reelection (Averich *et al.*, 1970, p. 161). In the meantime agrarian unrest among plantation laborers and tenant farmers has grown ever more explosive in the absence of fundamental reforms. The result may very well be that the Philippine party system has only bought temporary peace—a peace which requires ever larger amounts of cash, patronage, and virtuoso brokerage performances to maintain—while failing to tackle major social problems that will soon threaten the entire system. In the final analysis there are political issues that cannot be disposed of by machine-style bargaining and short-term payoffs—issues that require basic policy choices which the machine is ill-suited to make. Machine-style coordination may thus avoid short-run violence at the cost of maintaining basic structures that increase the long-run potential for revolutionary violence.

Depending as they do on particularistic, material incentives, the Nationalists and the Liberals—like machine parties elsewhere—are only as effective as their inducements. For portions of the modern sector where broader class loyalties and civic sentiments have begun to take root, or for the traditional sector where deference and symbolic goals are common, machine blandishments are likely to fall on barren soil. Machines therefore can manage conflict best among "transitional" populations and may be unable to alleviate strife—or may actually exacerbate it—in other social contexts.

CREATING LEGITIMACY

Urban American machines have long been credited with wedding the immigrant to the political system by protecting him, meeting his immediate needs, and offering *personal* (particularistic) service. To the immigrant the machine was legitimate in part because it accorded with his desire for a personal patron, usually from his own ethnic group, who stood ready to assist the humblest voter. But the machine gained legitimacy not only because of its warmth and familiarity; much of its legitimacy derived from its effectiveness in meeting the urgent daily material needs of thousands of clients. If it could no longer bring home the bacon, its electoral chances dimmed.

The new immigrants could be tied to the political system most easily through personal, material inducements, and the machine responded because each immigrant represented a potential vote which it needed. How effective such machine inducements were during the Boss Tweed era in New York City was underscored by what happened in the short reform period that followed his rule. Mandelbaum (1965, p. 106) states that, within only one year, reform mayor Havemeyer "did not have the support of a single mass based political organization." Reform governments, determined to avoid the corrupt practices of the machine, soon discovered that the cost of "clean" government was a marked loss of popular support. If the machine had stretched the city's finances to a point where its municipal bonds were no longer saleable, thereby jeopardizing its distributive capacity, the reform government's emphasis on fiscal austerity and the social distance of its leadership from most citizens quickly robbed it of its legitimacy.

In large multi-ethnic new states the favors a machine party can bring to its clientele may help preserve the territorial integrity of the state. Weiner (1967, pp. 71–72) claims, for example, that in India, where many ethnic groups are geographically concentrated, thus compounding the problem of alienation with that of secession, only machine-style bargaining and benefits, short of coercion, can hold the state together. The Congress Party did, in fact, increasingly distribute both particularistic rewards and pork-barrel projects whenever calls for regional autonomy reached threatening proportions, but the success of such efforts was spotty. Ironically, the desire for regional autonomy was prompted in part by a recognition that more civil service posts, more scholarships, and so forth would be available to the local party if regional autonomy were granted than if it were not.

The machine's latent function of building legitimacy is subject to the same qualification that was made for its capacity to settle conflict peacefully. Machine practices may engender support among those for whom material incentives are effective, but on the other hand they may increase the alienation of the new middle class, military officers, students, and the very traditional. Once again, *the impact of the inducement hinges on the social context.* The support generated by machine rewards, moreover, is based rather tenuously on the continuing distributive capacity of the regime. Lacking either ideological or charismatic foundations, the regime may find its support evaporating once it can no longer deliver the tangible inducements that serves as the party's social adhesive.

SHORT-RUN GOALS

In a sense the machine must buy its popularity. To the extent that it faces competition, the cost of popularity is raised and the public treasury may not be sufficient for the demands it must meet. The effect of this "squeeze" in urban America has often forced the machine party not only to raise the city's debt [2] but also to rely increasingly on assistance from businesses that

[2] Boss Tweed, in four years, raised New York City's indebtedness by a multiple of three while leaving both the tax rate and the assessments untouched. Mandelbaum, 1965, p. 77.

potentially have much to gain or lose from city decisions. This latter strategy was not without its penalities, as licenses and franchises were given to traction and power interests for negligible amounts and the city accepted substandard equipment and materials from influential contractors. *Frequently a three-cornered relationship developed in which the machine politicians could be viewed as brokers who, in return for financial assistance from business elites, promoted their policy interests when in office, while passing along a portion of the gain to a particularistic electorate from whom they "rented" their authority.* The substantial long-run costs to the community as a whole were seldom widely appreciated because the machine controlled an electorate with little sense of broad community interests and a preference for immediate, personal inducements.

Looked at in this way, the machine party facilitates a transaction between the poor and the rich. The poor trade their potential electoral power for wealth or security in the form of employment, help with the police, welfare, and bribes. The patronage and bribes distributed to the unorganized poor represent a "side-payment," moreover, which all but precludes basic structural change that might improve the *collective* access of the poor to economic opportunities and make those opportunities less ephemeral. Wealth elites, on the other hand, are trading their wealth for a measure of political influence over policy decisions that will, they anticipate, greatly enhance their future profits and commercial security. This transaction is a profoundly conservative one in that it provides the financial backers of the machine with an enormous influence over public policy.

Machines in new nations often have followed a similar pattern. The politicians who run such machines are the brokers in an alliance between commercial wealth on the one hand and a mass (but fragmented) electorate in urban or rural areas whose demands can be met particularistically on the other. Although the private sector occasionally was a less significant resource base than in urban America, the machine frequently developed close and occasionally secretive ties with commercial elites—especially in Southeast Asia and East Africa, where minority groups dominate the private sector. In nations such as Ghana, the party developed its most lucrative connections with large foreign firms rather than with indigenous capital, but the basic nature of the transaction was unchanged. The ruling party received much of its income from the private sector in return for protecting and advancing its patrons' various interests in policy, contracts, administrative decisions, and so forth. Meeting its reciprocal obligations to its financial backers and distributing material incentives for popular suport have made the machine's pursuit of longer-run development objectives all but impossible unless its material resources were expanded rapidly. Where revenue was not growing, many leaders dismantled electoral forms and turned to coercion to realize their vision of development. Elsewhere a dangerous running down of foreign exchange reserves or steeply inflationary deficits have been resorted to as fuel for the machine, thus eroding the financial base of the regime and focusing all efforts on short-term survival. Such regimes characteristically have been followed by military governments presiding over austerity programs.

NONCLASS FOCUS

The fact that the machine stresses family and parochial loyalties to the virtual exclusion of ideology and class politics requires little elaboration, as it is embedded in the definition of a machine.

> *So long as the public's interest continues to be centered on the scramble for particular benefits for individuals, overt rivalry will tend to be intraclass rather than interclass [Lande, 1965, p. 48].*

While it is true that older, high-status elites typically have looked askance at the possibilities for personal mobility provided to those of humbler origins by the machine, class issues of a collective nature beyond vague populism have been rare. Machines, by the nature of the rewards they offer and the personal ties they build into their organization, may well impede the growth of the class and occupational bonds implied by economic change, and thus may prolong the period during which family and/or ethnic ties are decisive.

An accurate assessment of the conservative effects of machine rule requires that one distinguish between a machine party's social base and the manner in which it aggregates interests. Only by making this distinction is it possible to understand how a regime which often finds its electoral strength among the lower classes can nevertheless pursue a basically conservative policy.

With regard to its social base, the machine party is essentially neutral. It links itself to those elements which can organize and deliver the votes on which it depends for victory. In portions of India, for example, the Congress Party has come to terms with locally powerful rajas and large landowners whom it had once opposed. In other areas where traditional leadership had eroded, the party based itself among commercialized, independent peasant proprietors or among the newly urbanized lower classes who had been organized by ambitious political brokers. The machine can thus adapt itself with some success to a variety of social strata, some of which are inherently conservative and some of which are potentially radical.

When it comes to the question of how interests are aggregated, however, the machine party is no longer either neutral—or very flexible. What a machine party does is to offer personal mobility (wealth, office) to its brokers who control significant "vote banks" and to provide them with the material resources for maintaining and delivering their votes on behalf of its candidates. The machine does not develop or respond to broad policy demands among its electoral clientele. Rather, it distributes particularistic, short-term rewards to a fragmented electorate so as to win at the polls while at the same time keeping its hands free in most policy matters. If the machine party's broad policy decisions are unaffected by its voting base so long as its capacity for doing favors remains strong, its policy decisions are most decidedly affected by the domestic or foreign commercial interests which provide much of its financial sinews. The social policy of a machine party—beyond the material favors it deploys to win elections—is thus apt to be more reflective of the interests of its financial base than of its electoral base.

It is conceivable that under certain circumstances the interests of the machine's financial patrons are more "progressive" than those of its voters. Early nineteenth-century England, where fairly traditional agrarian elites controlled more votes than the new commercial and industrial elites arising in the cities, might be such a case—as might the more traditional areas of India. For the most part, however, the effect of machine rule under universal suffrage is to submerge growing collective policy demands with immediate payoffs, thereby retarding the development of class-based political interests among the lower strata. The machine's lower-class voters are disaggregated and dealt with particularisticly while its upper-class financial backers and bureaucratic capitalists find their collective interests well cared for.

THE FAILURE OF THE MACHINE IN NEW NATIONS

Looking at politics in the new nations during the early 1960s, the machine model would have seemed an increasingly practical tool of analysis. Regimes that had begun with some popular legitimacy as heirs of the colonial regime and organizers of the nationalist movement were steadily losing much of the passionate, symbolic support they had once evoked. Yet at the same time, electoral forms retained enough vigor to reinforce the efforts of ruling parties to remain genuinely popular. Typically the ranks of the party had been swelled by many new members motivated by an understandable desire to acquire some influence in the new order. Politicization of the colonial bureaucracy was often underway and most parties were becoming adept at building support by distributing patronage, illegal favors, and pork-barrel projects. In spite of these harbingers of machine development, relatively few machine parties actually materialized and those that did were generally short-lived.

The task, therefore, is to explain why machines failed to develop as fully or as often as they did in urban America. The simplest answer, of course, is that embryonic machines in new nations generally were thrown out by military coups. Beyond this elementary truth, however, there are additional reasons why machine parties failed to flourish that relate directly to the social context of new nations and to the dynamics of machine politics itself.

The decline of machine politics in America is of only limited use in accounting for what happened to rudimentary machines in the new states. How, after all, does one compare the demise of two machines, one of which (the American) appears to die a more or less "natural" death, with a machine (that of the new nations) that is "assassinated" by a military coup?

Samuel Hays echoes the opinions of most analysts when he ascribes the atrophy and disappearance of the American urban machine to

> *certain rather obvious but momentous changes in American life. In the first place, a continually increasing majority of the active American electorate has moved above the poverty line. Most of this electorate is no longer bound to the party through the time-honored links of patronage and the machine. Indeed, for a large number of people, politics appears to have the character of an item of luxury consumption.*[3]

The services that tied the client to the machine either were no longer necessary or were performed by other agencies than the machine party. With aid to dependent children and old age assistance becoming the formal responsibility of the state and federal governments, "the precinct captain's hod of coal was a joke."[4] The protective and defensive functions of the machine party had simply ceased to be so important as political incentives.

Viewed from another angle, the machine simply destroyed its own social base. It had flourished among those who were, for one reason or another, "civic incompetents"; so when immigration slackened, when the new citizens gained a secure economic foothold and when they developed wider loyalties, the central prop of machine politics was destroyed. Here and there individual politicians managed to adapt to the new style and incentives, but the machine itself disappeared along with its social context.

[3] Samuel Hays, cited in Burnham, 1967, p. 305. To my knowledge, no actual empirical tests of hypotheses advanced for the rise or decline of machine politics have been attempted. It would be instructive, for example, to plot the growth and decline of machine-style politics over time in a number of American cities against possible explanatory variables such as rates of in-migration, changes in per-capita income, changes in income distribution, changes in welfare programs, rates of education, and so forth. I am grateful to Garry Brewer for suggesting this general line of inquiry.

[4] Banfield and Wilson, 1965, p. 121. The precinct captain still might be of some help in facilitating an application for welfare with a state agency, but the amount of help he could offer and the numbers of people for whom that assistance was important were both reduced.

The failure of machines in new nations not only differed from the American pattern, but varied somewhat from case to case according to the special circumstances of each nation. Nevertheless, we can discern a number of important factors that seem significant in the demise of many such embryonic machines. These factors related to (1) the stability of electoral forms; (2) the pattern of ethnic cleavage; (3) the economic resources of the party; and (4) the size of the potential machine clientele.

In the first place, the full development of a machine depends on its evolving capacity to create and maintain a large popular following with particularistic inducements. Typically, this capacity has developed best in the context of constant electoral pressures. Elections in American cities were virtually guaranteed by the fact that the city was a unit within a larger political system which sanctioned elections; machines perfected their techniques in the knowledge that they would surely face periodic electoral opposition. Ruling parties in new nations, however, often began with a considerable store of popularity generated in the nationalist period. As this enthusiasm deteriorated, the dominant party did not necessarily have to fall back on material incentives to retain its broad support; it could alternatively abrogate elections and escape the usual machine pressures. A good many nationalist leaders—having goals of transformation in mind—were increasingly discouraged at the growth of the particularistic demands from all quarters that liberal democratic forms seemed to foist upon them. Not having the heart for mediating between a host of what they considered short-sighted parochial demands, many leaders concluded that liberal democracy stood in the way of more vital, long-run, national goals. Both Nkrumah and Sukarno spoke feelingly in this regard, and both consciously chose to eschew elections and machine politics for more grandiose, symbolic goals.[5]

Another factor that basically altered the character of machines in some cases was the predominant position of a single ethnic group. In urban America it was seldom possible for a machine to rule without being obliged to knit together a broad coalition of ethnic groups. And the excluded groups, in any event, could rely on the protection afforded by stable rules of the game. Where the rules were more ephemeral and where machines could be based on one dominant ethnic group—e.g., pre-Ne Win Burma and, to a lesser extent, Nigeria—the excluded ethnic groups, which were often geographically concentrated, demanded more regional autonomy at the very

[5] In an otherwise perceptive article, Edward Feit (1968) characterizes, I think mistakenly, Nkrumah's CPP between 1962 and the military coup as a political machine. He distinguishes between a political party which "aggregates demands and converts them into legislative policy" and a political machine which "exists almost exclusively to stay in power." The problem, of course, is that many regimes are motivated almost solely to stay in power—e.g., the Thai military, Haiti's Duvalier—but the term "machine" should be reserved for civilian regimes which rest on a popular base. The CPP, until about 1960, can profitably be seen a machine party, but thereafter coercion and symbolic goals dominated.

least and actually launched secessionist revolts in some areas.[6] Not only did minority groups fear permanent exclusion from the benefits that government could confer, but they also feared the capacity of the dominant group to change the constitutional rules in order to destroy them or their culture.

Looking at those nations in which machine politics did develop with some vigor, the importance of the legitimacy of elections and of ethnic balance (or homogeneity) is manifest. Lebanon and India, for example, are sufficiently balanced ethnically so as to require some form of collaborative rule, and the Philippines is relatively homogeneous ethnically. No single group could easily dominate in the first two nations while, in the case of the Philippines, the major ethnic group is so overwhelmingly large that there are only a few minority groups, especially the Moslems, which feel threatened or excluded. All three had retained electoral forms as late as 1971. Beyond these two factors, however, are two broader obstacles to machine politics relating to its resource base and the nature of its clientele.

The resource base of successful machine parties in Asia and Africa became steadily more important after independence. Once the nationalist struggle was won the ruling party's support became ever more contingent upon the patronage it could distribute, the size of the government budget it had to work with, and the contributions it could elicit. A substantial loss of resources probably would entail the defection of some supporters, thereby jeopardizing the ruling party's coalition. Such defections were not so damaging to the party in the early independence period when its majorities were overwhelming, but it became a distinct threat as the nationalist coalition narrowed. William Riker (1962, pp. 39, 66) has attributed this paring down of "oversized coalitions" to the fact that the smaller a winning coalition is, the more spoils its members will share, whereas a huge winning majority may dilute winnings to the point of meaninglessness. Although such narrowing, in principle, would reduce the coalition to a bare majority, the uncertainties of political calculations in the new states prevented the process from extending that far. Some narrowing did occur, however, and its effect was to make the ruling party's majority increasingly vulnerable to the defections that a decline in its material resources might touch off. Whereas the party might earlier have survived such losses, they could well now mean the difference between victory and defeat.

A somewhat analogous process can be seen in the collapse of the Chicago Republican machine in the depression of the 1930s. Accustomed to a relatively abundant supply of material resources, the machine found itself in 1931 with a greatly reduced city treasury and fewer city jobs to dispense, with a huge drop in private contributions from streetcar and utility magnates such as Samuel Insull, and with little patronage at the county or state level

[6] For an excellent discussion of ethnic configurations and their political implications, see Geertz, 1963.

to fall back upon (Gosnell, 1968). The central role occupied by material resources in the form of city hall patronage and private-sector kickbacks was made evident to machine leaders who, competing without these advantages for the first time, were soundly beaten in the 1932 elections. Latent class and policy issues that had remained dormant as long as the machine had ample material rewards to distribute had reappeared with decisiveness.

Indications are that machines in new nations, like their American counterparts, require a large and steady *growth* in the volume of resources over time. What is more, as new participants learn of the advantages the government can confer, as the state extends its regulation over the economy, and as automatic loyalties erode, the cost of machine coordination grows. Machines in American cities tended, in fact, to live beyond their means, and the evidence suggests that machine parties in new nations behave similarly.[7] As a form of rule, then, machines are particularly subject to "an inflationary process of demand-formation" (Zolberg, 1966, p. 149) and naturally thrive best in an economy that provides them with a continually expanding store of material incentives to distribute.[8] Unlike American machines for which private-sector funds were often decisive, machines in Africa and Asia typically have been far more dependent on rewards such as patronage and contracts financed out of the national and local treasury. For such machines the volume of central government revenue was a key indicator of the ruling party's capacity to keep its electoral coalition intact without resort to coercion.

It is perhaps no coincidence that the high-water mark of machine politics in the new states occurred in the mid-1950s when Korean War boom prices for primary exports underwrote high rates of growth. In addition, there were a large number of "one-time-only" rewards available to ruling parties after independence: foreign businesses could be nationalized, new franchises and licenses could be let, expatriates and older civil servants could be replaced by loyal party workers. But in the absence of domestic economic expansion, the supply of such material incentives was soon exhausted. Assessing the instability of cabinet rule in Indonesia prior to Guided Democracy, Feith (1962, p. 572) concludes that

> *perhaps most fundamentally, the weakness of these later cabinets stemmed from their shortage of disposable rewards. . . . Moreover, the number of material rewards and prestige roles which government was expected to*

[7] This fact may indicate that machine politics is not a stable form of rule.

[8] The very success of machine parties in new nations in centrally distributing rewards and regulating the economy meant that when discontent came it was more likely both to be focused on the central government and to jeopardize the stability of central institutions.

> *provide did not decrease. . . . In sum, then, those cabinets were almost as poorly equipped to reward as to punish.*

It is reasonable to suppose that the Indonesian case is not unique. The material rewards were, finally, not sufficient to the task and, amid the ruling party's loss of support, the military—which, if it could not reward, could at least restrain and punish—stepped in.[9]

The collapse of embryonic machines in the late 1950s and early 1960s and their replacement by coercive parties or by the military in the new states can in large part be seen as a consequence of an economic pinch created by a slump in export prices for primary products and abetted by poorly performing local economies. At the time when their purses were contracting, however, many party machines were especially vulnerable. They had lost much of their charismatic authority, their own fiddling with electoral laws and preventive detention had undermined their legal claim to rule, and the idealism which the party's ennobling goals had once elicited was effaced by current stories of corruption by cabinet ministers.[10] The machine had thus become a rather profane institution at this point—one that depended almost exclusively on calculations of material advantage just when the material advantages it controlled were slipping away.

The general line of reasoning developed above suggests that the machine flourishes best at the subnational level, which is where it was confined in the United States. That is, *the durability of this political form is maximized where there is an external guarantor of the electoral process, where the machine is a part of a larger growing economy that can afford its expensive habits, and where its bosses do not have a monopoly of coercive authority.* A large measure of the instability of machines in developing nations may thus derive from their national rather than local character.[11]

Finally, in many nations economic pressures and demand inflation were not the only factors serving to weaken political machines; there was also some question of how well suited the social context was to machines. On the one hand, the machine faced opposition from a small but strategically placed upper middle class of civil servants, professionals, students, and, above all, army officers, which was much less amenable to material incentives and was, like its American counterpart, profoundly alienated by machine

[9] In a number of cases the military intervened only after the ruling party had itself forsaken electoral forms and had come to rely increasingly on coercion to retain its domination.

[10] It was at times like these that the American machine selected a "blue-ribbon" front man for mayor who would restore some legitimacy to the operation while allowing the party to remain in command behind the scenes.

[11] I am indebted to Henry Hart for suggesting this.

corruption and patronage.[12] On the other hand, these machines, particularly in Africa, faced large numbers of quite traditional folk for whom religious and cultural issues were still important [13] and whose leaders realized that the machine threatened the ascriptive basis of their power. As the state had not yet effectively penetrated many of these narrow political communities, their populations remained by and large outside the scope of machine incentives and represented, at a minimum, a latent challenge to the machine's authority. Bastions of tradition were often found in areas of "indirect rule" where colonial social and political change had been less severe. The machine, by contrast, won support especially among urban migrants and in areas (often "directly ruled") where folkways had been more uprooted by colonialism. The *transitional* population on which the machine relied was, in these cases, simply not large enough to sustain this form of government when it was menaced by widespread traditional recalcitrance and by a powerful middle class with military allies. Machines require not only an economy that performs tolerably well, but a social context that corresponds to the inducements it can deliver; only where both conditions have been satisfied have machines managed to survive.

[12] The fact that machines were typically of national scope in the new states of course made the army a key factor here.

[13] To stretch a point, one might link them with the forces in American politics that felt strongest about Sunday laws, prohibition, and so forth.

SELECTED BIBLIOGRAPHY

ABUEVA, JOSÉ VELOSO. 1966. "Conditions of Administrative Development: Exploring Administrative Culture and Behavior in the Philippines." Unpublished paper, Bloomington, Ind.: Comparative Administration Group.

ALMOND, GABRIEL, and J. BINGHAM POWELL. 1967. *Comparative Politics: A Developmental Approach.* Boston: Little, Brown & Co.

ANDERSON, EUGENE N., and PAULINE E. ANDERSON. 1967. *Political Institutions and Social Change in Continental Europe in the Nineteenth Century.* Berkeley and Los Angeles: University of California Press.

ANDRESKI, STANISLAV. 1968. *The African Predicament: A Study in the Pathology of Modernization.* London: Michael Joseph.

APTER, DAVID. 1968. "Nkrumah, Charisma and the Coup," *Daedalus,* XCVII, No. 3 (Summer), 757–792.

ARONSON, SIDNEY H. 1964. *Status and Kinship in the Higher Civil Service: Standards of Selection in the Administrations of John Adams, Thomas Jefferson, and Andrew Jackson.* Cambridge: Harvard University Press.

ASHTON, R. 1956. "Revenue Farming under the Early Stuarts," *Economic History Review,* 2nd Series, VIII, No. 3 (April).

AUSTIN, DENNIS. 1964. *Politics in Ghana: 1946–1960.* London: Oxford University Press.

AYLMER, G. E. 1961. *The King's Servants: The Civil Service of Charles I.* New York: Columbia University Press.

BAILEY, F. G. 1963. *Politics and Social Change: Orissa in 1959.* Berkeley and Los Angeles: University of California Press.

BANFIELD, EDWARD C. 1961. *Political Influence.* New York: The Free Press.

———, and JAMES A. WILSON. 1965. *City Politics.* Cambridge: Harvard University Press.

BATERINA, VIRGINIA F. 1955. "A Study of Money in Elections in the Philippines," *Philippine Social Sciences and Humanities Review,* XX, No. 1 (March), 36–96, and No. 2 (June), 137–212.

BAYLEY, DAVID H. 1960. "The Effects of Corruption in a Developing Nation," *Western Political Quarterly,* XIX (December).

BEER, SAMUEL. 1965. *British Politics in the Collectivist Age.* New York: Alfred A. Knopf, Inc.

BOISSEVAIN, JEREMY. 1966. "Patronage in Sicily." *Man,* I, No. 1 (March).

BOWEN, CATHERINE DRINKER. 1963. *Francis Bacon: The Temper of the Man.* Boston: Little, Brown & Co.

BRASS, PAUL R. 1965. *Factional Politics in an Indian State: The Congress Party in Uttar Pradesh.* Berkeley: University of California Press.

BRASZ, H. A. 1963. "Some Notes on the Sociology of Corruption," *Sociologica Neerlandica,* I, No. 2 (Autumn).

BRETTON, HENRY L. 1966. *The Rise and Fall of Kwame Nkrumah.* New York: Frederick A. Praeger, Inc.

BURNHAM, WALTER DEAN. 1967. "Party Systems and the Political Process." In William Nisbet Chambers and Walter Dean Burnham, eds., *The American Party System: Stages of Political Development.* New York: Oxford University Press, Inc., pp. 277–305.

CAMPBELL, J. K. 1964. *Honour, Family and Patronage: A Study of Institutions and Moral Values in a Greek Mountain Community.* Oxford: Clarendon Press.

CARMAN, HARRY J., and REINHARD H. LUTHIN. 1943. *Lincoln and the Patronage.* New York: Columbia University Press.

DAVIS, WILLIAM S. 1910. *The Influence of Wealth in Imperial Rome.* New York: The Macmillan Company.

DWIVEDY, SURENDRANATH, and G. S. BHARGAVA. 1967. *Political Corruption in India.* Delhi: Popular Book Services.

EDELMAN, MURRAY. 1964. *The Symbolic Uses of Politics.* Champaign-Urbana, Ill.: University of Illinois Press.

EISENSTADT, S. N. 1968. *Max Weber on Charisma and Institution Building.* Chicago and London: University of Chicago Press.

ELDERSVELD, SAM, *et al.* 1968. *The Citizen and the Administrator in a Developing Democracy.* Chicago: Scott, Foresman & Company.

FALL, BERNARD B. 1956. *The Viet-Minh Regime: Government and Administration in the Democratic Republic of Vietnam.* New York: Institute of Pacific Relations.

FALLERS, LLOYD. 1955. "The Predicament of a Modern African Chief," *American Anthropology,* LVII, 290–305.

FEIT, EDWARD. 1968. "Military Coups and Political Development: Some Lessons from Ghana and Nigeria," *World Politics,* XX (January), 179–193.

FEITH, HERBERT. 1962. *The Decline of Constitutional Democracy in Indonesia.* Ithaca, N.Y.: Cornell University Press.

———. 1967. "Dynamics of Guided Democracy." In Ruth T. McVey, ed., *Indonesia.* New Haven: Human Relations Area Files, pp. 309–409.

FITCH, BOB, and MARY OPPENHEIMER. 1966. *Ghana: The End of an Illusion.* New York: Monthly Review Press.

FLYNN, EDWARD J. 1947. *You're the Boss.* New York: The Viking Press, Inc.

FOSTER, GEORGE M. 1963. "The Dyadic Contract in Tzintzunzan, II: Patron Client Relationships," *American Anthropologist,* LXV, 1280–1294.

FRANDA, MARCUS. 1966. "The Political Idioms of Atulya Gosh," *Asian Survey,* VI (August), 420–433.

FRIEDRICH, C. J. 1966. "Political Pathology," *The Political Quarterly,* XXXVII (January–March).

FURNIVALL, J. S. 1960. *The Governance of Modern Burma.* New York: New York University Press.

GASH, NORMAN. 1953. *Politics in the Age of Peel: A Study in the Techniques of Parliamentary Representation, 1830–1850.* London: Longmans, Green & Company Ltd.

GEERTZ, CLIFFORD, ed. 1963. *Old Societies and New States.* New York: The Free Press.

GOLAY, FRANK H., *et al.* 1969. *Underdevelopment and Economic Nationalism in Southeast Asia.* Ithaca, N.Y.: Cornell University Press, Chap. 5, "Thailand."

GOSNELL, HAROLD F. 1968. *Machine Politics: Chicago Model.* 2nd ed. Chicago: University of Chicago Press.

GREENE, GRAHAM. 1966. *The Comedians.* New York: The Viking Press.

GREENSTONE, J. DAVID. 1966. "Corruption and Self-Interest in Kampala and Nairobi," *Comparative Studies in Society and History,* VIII, No. 2 (January), 199–210.

GWYN, WILLIAM B. 1962. *Democracy and the Cost of Politics in Britain.* London: The Athlone Press.

HEIDENHEIMER, ARNOLD J. 1963. "Comparative Party Finance: Notes on Practices and Toward a Theory." In Richard Rose and Arnold J. Heidenheimer, eds., "Comparative Studies in Political Finance: A Symposium," *Journal of Politics,* XXV, No. 4 (November), 790–811.

———. 1970. *Political Corruption: Readings in Comparative Analysis.* New York: Holt, Rinehart and Winston, Inc.

HILL, CHRISTOPHER. 1960. "The English Revolution: A Marxist Interpretation." In Philip Taylor, ed., *The Origins of the English Civil War.* Boston: D. C. Heath & Company.

HOFSTADTER, RICHARD. 1955. *The Age of Reform.* New York: Random House, Inc.

HOOGENBOOM, ARI. 1961. *Outlawing the Spoils: A History of the Civil Service Movement.* Urbana, Ill.: University of Illinois Press.

HUNTINGTON, SAMUEL P. 1968. *Political Order in Changing Societies.* New Haven: Yale University Press.

INSOR, D. 1963. *Thailand: A Political, Social and Economic Analysis.* New York: Frederick A. Praeger, Inc.

INTERNATIONAL BANK FOR RECONSTRUCTION AND DEVELOPMENT. 1959. *A Public Development Program for Thailand.* Baltimore: The Johns Hopkins Press.

KEY, V. O., JR. 1936. *The Techniques of Political Graft in the United States.* Chicago: University of Chicago Libraries.

LANDE, CARL H. 1965. *Leaders, Factions, and Parties—The Structure of Philippine Politics.* Monograph Series No. 6. New Haven: Southeast Asia Studies–Yale University.

LAPALOMBARA, JOSEPH. 1964. *Interest Groups in Italian Politics.* Princeton: Princeton University Press.

LEFF, NATHANIEL H. 1964. "Economic Development Through Bureaucratic Corruption," *American Behavioral Scientist* (November).

LEVI, CARLO. 1965. *Christ Stopped at Eboli.* New York: Pocket Books, Inc.

LEWIS, W. ARTHUR. 1965. *Politics in West Africa.* Toronto: Oxford University Press.

LEYS, COLIN. 1965. "What Is the Problem about Corruption?" *Journal of Modern African Studies,* III, No. 2, 215–230.

LOWI, THEODORE J. 1967. "Party, Policy, and Constitution in America." In William Nisbet Chambers and Walter Dean Burnham, eds., *The American Party System: Stages of Political Development.* New York: Oxford University Press, Inc., pp. 238–276.

MACKIE, J. A. C. 1967. *Problems of the Indonesian Inflation.* Monograph Series of the Cornell Modern Indonesia Project. Ithaca, N.Y.: Department of Asian Studies.

MCKITRICK, E. L. 1957. "The Study of Corruption," *Political Science Quarterly,* LXXII (December).

MCMULLEN, M. 1961. "A Theory of Corruption," *The Sociological Review* (Keele), IX (July).

MANDELBAUM, SEYMOUR. 1965. *Boss Tweed's New York.* New York: John Wiley & Sons, Inc.

MAUSS, MARCEL. 1954. *The Gift: Forms and Functions of Exchange in Archaic Societies.* New York: The Free Press.

MERRIAM, CHARLES E. 1929. *Chicago: A More Intimate View of Urban Politics.* New York: The Macmillan Company.

MILLER, ZANE L. 1969. *Boss Cox's Cincinnati.* New York: Oxford University Press, Inc.

MOUSNIER, ROLAND. 1945. *La Vénalité des offices sous Henri IV et Louis XIII.* Rouen: Editions Maugard.

MYRDAL, GUNNAR. 1968. *Asian Drama: An Inquiry into the Poverty of Nations.* New York: Pantheon Books, Inc.

NAMIER, SIR LEWIS. 1961. *England in the Age of the American Revolution*. London: Macmillan & Co., Ltd.

NASH, MANNING. 1966. "Tradition and Tension in Kelantan," *Journal of Asian and African Studies,* I (June), 310–314.

NEEDLER, MARTIN C. 1961. "The Political Development of Mexico," *American Political Science Review,* LV, No. 2 (June), 308–312.

NICHOLAS, RALPH W. 1963. "Village Factions and Political Parties in Rural West Bengal," *Journal of Commonwealth Political Studies,* II (November).

"North Vietnam: A Special Survey," *The China Quarterly,* IX (January–March), 2–111.

NYE, J. S. 1967. "Corruption and Political Development: A Cost-Benefit Analysis," *American Political Science Review,* LXI, No. 2 (June).

O'BRIEN, C. C. 1957. *Parnell and His Party*. London: Oxford University Press.

PAGÈS, G. 1932. "La Vénalité des offices dans l'ancienne France," *Révue Historique,* CLXIX, 477–495.

PYE, LUCIAN W. 1962. *Politics, Personality and Nation Building: Burma's Search for Identity*. New Haven: Yale University Press.

———. 1967. *Southeast Asia's Political Systems*. Englewood Cliffs, N.J.: Prentice-Hall, Inc.

Report of the Commission [of Enquiry into NADECO Ltd.] *Appointed under the Commission of Enquiry Act, 1964* (S. Azu Crabbe, Chairman). 1966. Accra: Government of Ghana (August).

Report of the Commission of Enquiry into the Affairs of the Cocoa Purchasing Co. Ltd. ["Jibowu Commission"]. 1956. Accra: Government Printers.

Report of the Commission of Enquiry into the Matter of Pratap Singh Kairon ["Das Commission"]. 1964. New Delhi: Government Printer (June 11).

Report of the Committee on the Prevention of Corruption ["Santhanam Report"]. 1964. New Delhi: Ministry of Home Affairs.

Report of the Corporation of Calcutta Enquiry Commission ["Talukdar Committee Report"]. 1962. Calcutta: Government of West Bengal.

Report of the Railway Corruption Enquiry Committee ["Kripilani Committee"], *1953–1955*. 1955. Delhi: Government of India, Ministry of Railways.

RIGGS, FRED W. 1962. "Interest and Clientele Groups." In Joseph L. Sutton, ed., *Problems of Politics and Administration in Thailand*. Bloomington, Ind.: Institute of Training for Public Service, pp. 153–192.

———. 1963. "Bureaucrats and Political Development: A Paradoxical View." In Joseph LaPalombara, ed., *Bureaucracy and Political Development*. Princeton: Princeton University Press, pp. 120–167.

———. 1964. *Administration in Developing Countries*. Boston: Houghton Mifflin Company.

———. 1966. *Thailand: The Modernization of a Bureaucratic Polity*. Honolulu: East-West Center Press.

RIKER, WILLIAM. 1962. *The Theory of Political Coalitions*. New Haven: Yale University Press.

RIORDEN, WILLIAM L. 1963. *Plunkett of Tammany Hall*. New York: E. P. Dutton Co.

ROGOW, ARNOLD A., and HAROLD D. LASSWELL. 1963. *Power, Corruption and Rectitude*. Englewood Cliffs, N.J.: Prentice-Hall, Inc.

ROSE, RICHARD, and ARNOLD J. HEIDENHEIMER, eds. 1963. "Comparative Studies in Political Finance: A Symposium," *Journal of Politics,* XXV, No. 4 (November).

ROSENBERG, HANS. 1958. *Bureaucracy, Aristocracy, and Autocracy: The Prussian Experience, 1660–1815.* Boston: Beacon Press, Inc.

SCOTT, JAMES C. 1968. *Political Ideology in Malaysia: Reality and the Beliefs of an Elite.* New Haven: Yale University Press.

———. 1967. "An Essay on the Political Functions of Corruption," *Asian Studies,* V (December).

———. 1969a. "The Analysis of Corruption in Developing Nations," *Comparative Studies in Society and History,* II (June).

———. 1969b. "Corruption, Machine Politics and Political Change," *American Political Science Review,* LXIII (December).

———. 1972 (*in press*). "Patron-Client Politics and Political Change in Southeast Asia," *American Political Science Review* (March).

SEGAL, RONALD. 1965. *The Crisis of India.* London: Jonathan Cape Ltd.

SHOR, EDGAR L. 1962. "The Public Service." In Joseph L. Sutton, ed., *Problems of Politics and Administration in Thailand.* Bloomington, Ind.: Institute of Training for Public Service, pp. 23–40.

SIFFIN, WILLIAM J. 1966. *The Thai Bureaucracy: Institutional Change and Development.* Honolulu: East-West Center Press.

SILCOCK, T. H., ed. 1967. *Thailand: Social and Economic Studies in Development.* Durham, N.C.: Duke University Press.

———, and H. D. EVERS. 1967. "Elites and Selection." In T. H. Silcock, ed., *Thailand: Social and Economic Studies in Development.* Durham, N.C.: Duke University Press, pp. 84–104.

SILVERMAN, SYDEL F. 1965. "Patronage and Community Relationships in Central Italy," *Ethnology,* IV.

SKINNER, G. WILLIAM. 1958. *Leadership and Power in the Chinese Community of Thailand.* Ithaca, N.Y.: Cornell University Press.

SOUKUP, JAMES R. 1963. "Japan." In Richard Rose and Arnold J. Heidenheimer, eds., "Comparative Studies in Political Finance: A Symposium," *Journal of Politics,* XXV, No. 4 (November), 737–756.

STEFFENS, LINCOLN. 1963. *The Shame of the Cities.* New York: Hill & Wang, Inc.

SUTTON, JOSEPH L., ed. 1962. *Problems of Politics and Administration in Thailand.* Bloomington, Ind.: Institute of Training for Public Service.

SWART, K. W. 1949. *Sale of Office in the Seventeenth Century.* The Hague: Martinus Nijhoff.

TAWNEY, R. H. 1958. *Business and Politics under James I.* London: Cambridge University Press.

TAYLOR, LILY ROSS. 1961. *Party Politics in the Age of Caesar.* Berkeley: University of California Press.

TAYLOR, PHILIP, ed. 1960. *The Origins of the English Civil War.* Boston: D. C. Heath & Company.

TILMAN, ROBERT O. 1968. "Emergence of Black-Market Bureaucracy: Administration, Development, and Corruption in the New States," *Political Administration Review,* XXVIII, No. 5 (September–October), 437–444.

TREVOR-ROPER, H. R. 1962. "The Gentry—1540–1640," *Economic History Review,* Supplement 1. London: Cambridge University Press.

WALCOTT, ROBERT, JR. 1956. *English Politics in the Early Eighteenth Century.* Cambridge: Harvard University Press.

WALDBY, H. O. 1950. *The Patronage System of Oklahoma.* Norman, Okla.: The Transcript Co.

WEBER, MAX. 1947. *The Theory of Social and Economic Organization,* ed. Talcott Parsons. New York: The Free Press.

WEINER, MYRON. 1962. *The Politics of Scarcity.* Chicago: University of Chicago Press.

———. 1967. *Party Building in a New Nation: The Indian National Congress.* Chicago: University of Chicago Press.

WERTHEIM, W. F. 1965. *East-West Parallels.* Chicago: Quadrangle Books.

WILSON, DAVID A. 1962. *Politics in Thailand.* Ithaca, N.Y.: Cornell University Press.

WILSON, JAMES Q. 1961. "The Economy of Patronage," *Journal of Political Economy* (August), 369–380.

WRAITH, RONALD, and EDGAR SIMPKINS. 1963. *Corruption in Developing Countries.* London: George Allen & Unwin Ltd.

WURFEL, DAVID. 1963. "The Philippines." In Richard Rose and Arnold J. Heidenheimer, eds., "Comparative Studies in Political Finance: A Symposium," *Journal of Politics,* XXV, No. 4 (November), 757–773.

ZELDEN, THEODORE. 1958. *The Political System of Napoleon III.* London: Macmillan & Co. Ltd.

ZINK, HAROLD. 1930. *City Bosses in the United States.* Durham, N.C.: Duke University Press.

ZOLBERG, ARISTIDE. 1966. *Creating Political Order: The Party States of West Africa.* Chicago: Rand McNally & Co.

INDEX